SEEN AND NOT HEARD

A garland of fancies

for Victorian children

Selected and introduced by
NIGEL TEMPLE

Hutchinson of London

HUTCHINSON & CO (*Publishers*) LTD
178-202 Great Portland Street, London W1

London Melbourne Sydney
Auckland Johannesburg Cape Town
and agencies throughout the world

First published 1970

Designed by Georgina Bannister

© Nigel Temple 1970

*This book has been set in Old Style Series 2, printed in
Great Britain on antique wove paper by
Taylor Garnett Evans & Co. Ltd., Lithographic Printers,
Greycaine Road, Bushy Mill Lane, Watford, Herts.,
and bound by Wm. Brendon, of Tiptree, Essex*

ISBN 0 09 104040 X

I acknowledge a debt to the many writers and illustrators –
known and anonymous – who left so great a wealth of
instructive and entertaining material, and to my wife, Judith,
who wrote the sectional introductions.

Several of the books represented in this anthology are undated.
But whenever the year of publication of a book is known, it
has been printed below the extract concerned.

N.H.L.T.

CONTENTS

Preface

The field for *Seen and Not Heard* has been narrowed by design and chance. First, all extracts have been taken from works in my own collection of *illustrated* nineteenth-century juvenile books. Then, from these, only those printed between 1837 and about 1880 have been considered. This anthology is, then, idiosyncratic and not a balanced choice from a number of national collections. The need for varieties of style, form and content has had its influence. No place has been given to works of fantasy and fairyland, Empire adventure and global exploration, or historical tales and contemporary classics. Alphabets, numerators and textbooks, all with their special appeals and relevance, are excluded, as are never-never-land illustrations and, for example, the age-less creations of Kate Greenaway, the anthropomorphisms of Charles Bennett and the nonsense of Edward Lear.

In fact, the only material included appeared in the first forty-five years of Victoria's reign, mostly in common-place illustrated books, offering us some sort of insight into the life and times of Victorian children: material prepared, of course, by adults on matters and in a manner which they deemed fit for their young ones to read and look at.

Readers who anticipate a collection of unfamiliar literary masterpieces will be disappointed. They might find that occasional naively charming passage and almost certainly discover much that was previously unknown to them. Very few of the extracts appear to have been reproduced elsewhere and many of the books have not been documented previously for publication, presumably having been unnoticed or not considered of sufficient significance to record in print.

Yet books such as these (quite apart from their value to collectors interested in the development of printing, binding design, illustration and publishing), must have had influence in their time. They were sold and given in great numbers to the newly-literate masses and their distribution was not limited to Sunday School prize-winners in dismal industrial back streets. Some, like the earlier factual Peter Parley's Annuals (1840–1888), were sophisticated products aimed at the child with some formal education behind him. Other books, through Missions and schools, reached the outposts of the Empire.

Some of the books quoted were written before 1837 and remained popular, to be re-published in various forms later in the century. *Original Poems*, for example, which appeared first in 1804–05 for Darton, Harvey and Darton, was re-published in new form by George Routledge in 1868. The latter is quoted.

Children's books, often loaded with thinly veiled religious doctrine, were products of what was still relatively a manual industry early in our period. By the '80s, evangelical zeal and industrial progress had revolutionised production. Such bodies as the long-established S.P.C.K. (Church of England), and the R.T.S. (unsectarian), were prolific publishers. They, with other organisations such as The Church Missionary Society, The Sunday School Union, Protectors of Animals and Children, Temperance Societies and Slavery Abolitionists, had promoted a phenomenal quantity of publications – books, tracts, maga- zines and annuals – to propagate their beliefs among infant minds.

The chapters of *Seen and Not Heard* are arranged in various ways. *Hearth and Home* is in two sections – parents and children, followed by home scenes. *High Days and Holidays* follows the annual cycle. *Sickness and Death* deals first with the grave, then sickness and finally death.

Some illustrations relate directly to specific extracts, but most of them stand independently as visual expansions of the text. They represent the work of various artists and engravers and a range of graphic processes. Most are from wood- engravings. None are photographic in origin. Lithography, steel-engraving, hand-colouring and the Kronheim process are reproduced.

As wood blocks were easily cut down and re-used for a different edition or format, or even for several titles, they tended to become worn and were repaired over the years. They might also become anonymous, losing the artist's and the engraver's name as a result of reducing the size of block. Illustrations are not, therefore, necessarily contemporaneous with the books in which they appear.

All works quoted or illustrated appear in the Bibliography, which it is hoped will be useful to the collector as well as of service to the general reader. It gives fuller details of books than appear below extracts and with illustrations.

The older reader will not be astonished by some of the dogmas, presumptions and social customs revealed by the text.

Preface

Younger generations may find some of the attitudes, manners and social relationships implicit or explicit in almost every paragraph quite incredible. Yet few people could deny that they see something of themselves here; perhaps more clearly still the attitudes and prejudices of others.

It is hoped that readers of *Seen and Not Heard* will find entertainment and arrive at a more intimate understanding of an age separated from our own by so few generations (a living ninety-five-year-old could have read some of these books on their day of publication), yet which is so different from it in outlook and way of life.

Finally, to quote verses by E.S.H.B., from *The Children's Friend*, June, 1865:

Ah! here is a truly nice present!
A book full of pictures and tales;
How pretty and graceful this drawing,
A ship, with her rigging and sails.

Here's a man who seems wounded and ill,
Two merry boys running a race,
A little girl put in the corner,
With downcast and cross-looking face.

'True courage,' or, 'Who is the coward?'
'The midshipman's first trip to sea.'
'How little Kate nursed her sick mother.'
'The rosebud, the wind, and the bee.'

'The life of old Jack, the tame monkey,'
I think that seems full of great fun,
And still there are more illustrations,
With stories to every one.

I know you are longing to hear them,
But then I have so much to do,
That I must away to my business,
And cannot stay longer with you.

Preface

I wish you'd make haste with your learning,
And not be dependent on me,
To find out and tell you the meaning
Of each pretty picture you see.

When once you can read all these pages,
And not, like a baby, just look,
You'll gain a large store of amusement,
And really enjoy your nice book.

Cheltenham   N.H.L.T.

HEARTH & HOME

With Victoria and Albert setting the sublime example, the middle class family's ethics and daily routine were as predictable as the Sabbath. Its self-sufficiency and complacency were as yet unruffled by conflicting influences and outside controls. Discipline must have been a simple matter for these flawless parents whose Evangelical morality gave all the answers. A simple appeal to conscience was enough to bring the most wayward child to heel. It wasn't that blood was thicker than water – Duty was the foundation of all family relationships.

Natural childish instincts were seen as temptations to resist. Every attempt to deviate from conformity was to be thwarted by a stricken conscience. Virtue was its own reward, and even praise was faint because Aspiration meant more than Achievement.

The consequences of social misbehaviour and venial sins were almost as dire as those of the mortal ones: 'want of openness' and disobedience. For whatever you did wrong, you offended either God, or, almost as bad, your parents.

Childhood seems to have been a condition to grow out of and master. In later story books, children were to have proper adventures that had nothing to do with behaviour. But the mid-Victorian fictional child could never escape from the clutches of his parents or his conscience.

The ideal home was a hive of cut and dried zeal and profitable activity. Even fun had to be purposeful. All was dedicated to high thinking and cosy living. Where was the mystery and magic of childhood?

My Father

Dear Father, while daily and hourly I see
New proofs of your tender affection for me;
It may please you to know how your kindness has won
The return that it calls for – the love of a son.

Some fathers are distant, and stern, and severe,
They speak to command, and they govern by fear;
Obedience, indeed, by such means may be won,
But they fail in securing the love of a son.

Your praise, my dear Father, is easy to earn,
When you teach me, I feel it a pleasure to learn;
And when tasks are concluded, and duties are done,
You share in the pastimes and sports of your son.

I am often unthinking and idle, 'tis true,
But I freely confess all my follies to you;
You tell me what ways to pursue and to shun,
And you leniently look on the faults of your son.

Relax not your cares, dearest Father, I pray,
I shall need your kind counsels through life's busy way;
Continue the system so wisely begun,
And still be the friend and the guide of your son.

MRS ABDY *Green's Nursery Album*, 1848

My Mother

Mother, again I see you stand
Amid your prattling infant band;
Again, in haste, aside you lay
The book you wished to read to day:
Your time is given to us alone,
Scarcely a moment seems your own;
Where shall we ever find another
To care for us like you, my Mother?

You wisely train each well-loved child,
Gently you chide the rash and wild,
You tenderly support the meek,
And give protection to the weak;
I know that we are deemed to be
A fond, united family;
Your influence binds us to each other:
We owe our peace to you, my Mother.

Dear Mother! at a future day,
May we your ceaseless love repay;
Each hour may we recall in thought
The virtuous lessons you have taught,
And if enticed to go astray,
Oh! may we to our tempters say –
'The way we tread shall be no other
'Than that first shown us by our Mother.'

MRS ABDY   *Green's Nursery Album, 1848*

Obedience to Parents

Let children that would fear the Lord
Hear what their teachers say:
With reverence hear their parent's word,
And with delight obey.

Have you not heard what dreadful plagues
Are threaten'd by the Lord,
To him that breaks his father's laws,
Or mocks his mother's word?

What heavy guilt upon him lies!
How cursed is his name!
The ravens shall pick out his eyes,
And eagles eat the same.

But those that worship God, and give
Their parents honour due,
Here on this earth they long shall live,
And live hereafter too.

ISAAC WATTS *Divine and Moral Songs for Children*

The Clock of Life

'And now, Lewis,' said Mr Rollins, 'that you have learned to
know the hour by the clock in the hall, I must draw your
attention to another clock – the clock of life; I mean the beating of your pulse; for it may often remind you of the value of
time, and the necessity of turning it to good account. Time is
worth more than finest gold.

'My pulse is the clock of my life;
It shows how my moments are flying;
It marks the departure of time,
And tells me how fast I am dying.'

'I will show you how to lay the tip of your finger on your
pulse properly, and you must remember that at every beat you
have lived a moment longer in the world, and have a moment
less to live in it. Truly may we all say, "Lord, make me to know

PROVERBS
Above: A soft answer
Below: Hearken unto thy father
From *The Proverbs of Solomon* (one of 'Aunt Louisa's Sunday
Books')

mine end, and the measure of my days, what it is; that I may
know how frail I am. Behold, thou hast made my days as an
hand-breadth; and mine age is as nothing before Thee."
Psalm XXXIX, 4, 5.'
A dozen times in the course of that day was Lewis running
into the hall to look at the clock; and as many times was he
heard to repeat the words, while the tip of his finger was on
his wrist –

'My pulse is the clock of my life;
It shows how my moments are flying;
It marks the departure of time,
And tells me how fast I am dying.'

ANON   *The Children's Friend*, October 1868

Uttering a Falsehood

During the brief moments that followed the exclamation of
Edward, Harry resolved on the attempt to hide his dishonesty
under the flimsy veil of untruth. 'Papa,' he said, 'papa did not
give me my weekly money.'
'How dare you tell a falsehood of your own father, sir!'
exclaimed Mr Blount, who had heard the assertion from behind
the arbour, and who seized his son by the collar at the same
instant that he spoke. 'How dare you utter a falsehood? Did
I not see you stake your sixpence, after the commands I have
so often repeated, that you should never play cards for money?
And then to vent your ill-humour upon an affectionate animal
that sought to caress you! Begone, sir, and hide your face, for
your own father is ashamed to look upon you – begone!'
The sinful and abashed boy hung down his head, as well he
might, in sorrow and in shame. It was in vain that his young
friends interceded for him – it was in vain that Mr Millar begged
his father would forgive this his first offence. Mr Blount was too
much displeased to palliate his fault; and Harry retired to his
own chamber to mourn the results of his evil propensity.

MRS S. C. HALL   *The Juvenile Budget*, 1840

Aunt Ross's Social Lesson

Nothing, however, is more difficult than to define what it is to be genteel and fashionable. Aunt Ross thought she was a perfect judge on these important subjects; but many other fashionable ladies would have laughed at Aunt Ross's notions, and considered her a vulgar under-bred woman; while, perhaps, these very ladies themselves would, in their turn, be held in scorn by others. One of Aunt Ross's methods of forming, as she said, the manners of her young people, was to make them pass two hours in the drawing-room on those forenoons when she remained at home, to receive such visitors as might happen to call. It was for this purpose that Anna was now desired to follow her aunt to the drawing-room. On arriving there, Anna and her cousin were desired to seat themselves in a window, and occupy their time in getting a lesson for their Italian master; but when any person called to whom Aunt Ross introduced them, to be attentive in remarking their manners, their style of address, and so on. 'If I do not introduce you to any visitor, Anna,' said Aunt Ross, 'you may suppose that I do not wish you to imitate the manners of that person, and you may just go on with your lesson.' Such were Aunt Ross's instructions; and Anna was thinking them over, that she might be ready to obey them, when a servant opened the drawing-room door, and announced 'Mrs Elford,' and a pleasing-looking elderly lady entered.

'Mrs Elford! How do you do?' said Aunt Ross, but without seeming very happy to see her. 'How is Mr Elford, and your young people?'

'All well, thank God,' replied Mrs Elford; and then looking smilingly to Anna and Louisa, 'I hope you are both well, my dears?'

Anna, who had been taught by her Mamma, that the only way to be truly polite was to obey God's command, to love every one, and to feel gratified for every mark of kindness from others, immediately rose and hastened to give her hand to Mrs Elford, and looked pleased and grateful for her notice, while Louisa did not venture to leave her seat, till her Mamma said coldly, 'Come and speak to Mrs Elford, my dear.' She then approached, but Mrs Elford did not seem now to observe her, being wholly occupied with Anna. She had drawn the grateful looking, smiling little orphan, into her kind bosom, and was now caressing her as she talked to her, while a tear sometimes stood in her eye.

INDOOR GARDENING.

'Will you come and see me, my love? I have many young people at home, and I am sure they will all be most happy to see you.'

'I shall like very much to come, I am sure,' replied Anna, drawing the kind Mrs Elford's hand closer round her waist, 'if aunt will allow me.'

'I allow of very little visiting,' said Aunt Ross, dryly, 'but we shall think about it; and now you may return to your lessons.'

Anna was again kissed by Mrs Elford, and then obeyed her aunt.

When the two little girls had resumed their seats, Mrs Elford asked Mrs Ross in what church she had decided to take a pew.

'Not in the one you advised, Mrs Elford,' replied Mrs Ross. 'I found, on inquiry, that scarcely any genteel people sat there.'

'I did not say genteel people sat there,' replied Mrs Elford; 'I said the gospel was purely preached there; and the clergyman so plain in his style, and at the same time so attractive

and persuasive in his manner, that I thought your young
people would love him, and listen with attention to him, as I
find mine do.'
'Oh, I hope my young people are too well instructed not to
listen to any clergyman their parents take them to hear,'
replied Aunt Ross, 'but I do not choose them to go where so
few genteel people think of going. I have decided on taking a
pew either in St George's Church, or in one of the Church of
England Chapels; but I think the latter, because, though I
understand St George's is crowded with the genteelest people,
I am told the clergyman is very uncharitable in his style of
preaching, always addressing even his congregation as if they
were irreligious people, which I think is quite contrary to the
mildness and charity inculcated by the Christian religion.'
Mrs Elford was beginning to answer Aunt Ross, when the
door was again thrown open, and the servant announced 'Lady
Alderston,' and Mrs Ross was immediately in such a bustle to
receive this, as she thought, fashionable visitor, that she
seemed quite to forget Mrs Elford. That good lady, however,
quietly rose to take leave, and, before going, went to the
window where the little girls were sitting, again kindly invited
Anna to visit her; and then, taking a pretty little book from
her pocket, gave it to her, saying, 'Ask your aunt's leave, my
love, and then read this little book. I am sure you will like it.'
Anna thanked Mrs Elford very gratefully, and then, though
she longed very much to look at the kind lady's gift, she put it
aside till she should ask her aunt's leave.
It had taken all this time for Lady Alderston to come upstairs. At last she entered – a lady so fat, she seemed scarcely
able to walk, dressed out in the most fantastic style, and
accompanied by a little dog quite as fat, which came into the
room puffing and wheezing, and immediately squatted itself
down on the rug. Lady Alderston sunk down on a sofa; and
Mrs Ross called to Louisa to bring a foot-stool, and herself
placed a cushion; and at last the poor lady seemed tolerably
comfortable.
'Allow me to introduce my niece to you, my dear Lady
Alderston,' said Aunt Ross, looking toward Anna, who
immediately approached. Lady Alderston looked carelessly at
her for a moment.
'A fine child, Mrs Ross. Pray, have you got the French
governess you were in quest of?' and she took no more notice

of Anna, who returned to her seat in the window rather morti-
fied, but recollecting her aunt's injunction to pay particular
attention to the manners of those to whom she was introduced.
Lady Alderston spoke of the theatre, and of parties, and of
balls, and of young ladies who had come out, and of Lord this,
and Lord that, and Sir John and Sir Thomas, and Lady M——
and Lady S——, the one's carriage, and the other's beautiful
suite of rooms. And Mrs Ross seemed delighted, and poor
Anna listened as she desired, while her little face became
colourless, and she yawned every minute, and was at last quite
happy to hear another visitor announced, and then another,
and another; but Lady Alderston sat on, and she still was
obliged to listen. She was introduced by her aunt to several
other visitors; but the two hours in the drawing-room seemed
to Anna the longest she had ever spent in her life, and she felt
quite rejoiced when her aunt permitted her and Louisa to
return to the schoolroom. As they went Louisa whispered to
her, 'You know, Anna, we are to imitate Lady Alderston, now
see how well I can obey Mamma;' and then she walked exactly
like her, imitating every motion, till she reached the school-
room door. She threw it open, and called out 'Lady Alderston,'
and then waddled into the room, and sunk down on a chair,
pretending to pant for breath, as she had done. Anna could not
help laughing, yet she felt that she was wrong in doing so, for
her Mamma had often told her that those who ridiculed others
for personal defects, which they could not help, mocked not
at them, but at their Creator.

GRACE KENNEDY *Anna Ross*, 1848

Honouring Parents

No worse sign of a child's character can appear than a readiness
to speak lightly of a parent's authority. The great God who
made heaven and earth, and can make good all He says, looks
upon disobedience to parents as one of the most grievous sins
a child can commit, and pronounces a dreadful curse upon it.

ANON *The Children's Friend*, November 1868

The Clever Boy

'Well, but grandmama!' expostulated Edwin, 'everybody says I am very clever; now do not laugh, everybody says so, and what everybody says must be true.'

'First,' replied his grandmother, 'I do not think that what everybody says must of necessity be true; and, secondly, in what consists your "everybody?" '

'Why, there is nurse.'

'Capital authority! an old woman who nursed your mother, and, consequently, loves *you* dearly; go on.'

'And the doctor; he said I was so clever, the other morning, when I swallowed the pill without one crooked face.'

'Go on.'

'All the servants.'

'Excellent servants, Edwin, for the situations they are engaged to fill, but bad judges of a young gentleman's cleverness. The Rector – ?'

'That is cruel of you, grandmama,' replied our conceited little friend; 'you know he would not say it, because I did not get through the Commandment in the class last Wednesday evening.'

'Does your papa say you are clever?'

The little fellow made no reply.

'Do your schoolfellows?'

'They are all big boys.'

'Then your character for cleverness depends on the old nurse, the still older doctor, and the servants!'

Edwin was again silent.

MRS S. C. HALL   *Green's Nursery Album*, 1848

Trouble with Servants

Soon after my husband and I went in, while we were sitting in the parlour, Mrs Jones had occasion to call a servant. I noticed that, when she rang the bell, she did so with a quick jerk; and I could perceive a tone of authority in the tingling of the bell, the sound of which was distinctly heard. Nearly two minutes passed before the servant made her appearance, in which time the bell received a more vigorous jerk. At last she entered, looking flushed and hurried.

Trouble with Servants

'What's the reason you did not come when I first rang?' inquired our lady hostess, in a severe tone.

'I – I – came as quick as I could,' replied the girl, with a look of mortification at being spoken to before strangers.

'No, you didn't! It's your custom to wait until I ring twice. Now let this be the last time!'

And then, in a low voice, Mrs Jones gave the direction for which she had summoned her.

'Such a set!' ejaculated the lady, as the girl left the room. Her words were intended to reach other ears besides ours; and so they did. 'That girl,' she continued, addressing me, 'has a habit of making me ring twice. It really seems to give them pleasure, I believe, to annoy one. Ah, me! this trouble with servants is never-ending. It meets you at every turn.'

And for some time she launched out upon her favourite theme – for such it appeared to be – until her husband, who was evidently annoyed, managed to change the subject. Once or twice she came back to it before tea-time.

At last the tea-bell rang, and we ascended to the dining-room. We were just seated, when a frown suddenly darkened the brow of our hostess, and her hand applied itself nervously to the table-bell.

The girl who had set the table came up from the kitchen. 'There is no sugar in the bowl,' said Mrs Jones sharply. 'I wish you would learn to set the table while you are about it. I'm sure I've spoken to you often enough.'

As the girl took the sugar-bowl to fill it, the frown left the face of our hostess, and she turned to me with a bland smile, and asked whether I took sugar and cream. I replied in the affirmative; but did not smile in return, for I could not. I knew the poor girl's feelings were hurt at being spoken to in such a way before strangers, and this made me extremely uncomfortable.

'Do you call this cream?' was the angry interrogation of Mrs Jones, as the girl returned with the sugar, pushing towards her the cream-jug, which she had lifted from the table as she spoke.

'Yes ma'am,' was the reply.

'Look at it, and see, then.'

'It's the cream,' said the girl.

'If that's cream, I never want to see milk. Here! take it away and bring me the cream.'

The girl looked confused and distressed. But she took the cream-jug and went down stairs with it.

'That's just the way they always do!' said Mrs Jones, leaning back in her chair. 'I really get out of all patience sometimes.'

In a little while the girl returned.

'It's the cream, ma'am, as I said. Here's the milk.' And she presented two vessels.

Mrs Jones took both from her hands with an ill-natured jerk. It was as the girl had said.

'Such cream!' fell from the lips of our hostess, as she commenced pouring it into the cups already filled with tea.

The girl went down stairs to take back the milk she had brought up, but she was scarcely at the bottom of the stairs, when the bell was rung for her.

'Why don't you stay here? What are you running off about?' said Mrs Jones, as she came in hurriedly. 'You know I want you to wait on the table.'

And so it was during the whole meal. The girl was not once spoken to except in a tone of anger or offensive authority.

I was no longer surprised that Mrs Jones found it difficult to keep good domestics, for no one of feeling can long remain with a woman who speaks to them always in a tone of command, or who reproves them in the presence of visitors.

My husband was very severe upon Mrs Jones after we returned home. 'No lady,' said he, 'ever spoke in anger or reproof to a domestic before a visitor or stranger. Nothing more surely evinces a vulgar and unfeeling mind.'

T. S. ARTHUR *Homes Scenes and Home Influences*, 1866

No Place for Prayer

The mother of a little boy about six years of age, some time ago went in search of a house, taking her son along with her. Having taken one of but a single apartment, on their way home the boy burst into tears. His mother inquired what was the matter. 'Because you have taken that house,' said the child. 'My dear,' replied the mother, 'is not that a better house than the one which we at present occupy?'

'Yes,' said the little boy, sobbing, 'but there is no closet for *prayer* in it.'

How few, when taking houses, look out for such conveniences!

ANON   *The Children's Friend*, June 1868

Family Prayer

Come, little John, come and sit with me; I want to tell you something. I am not going to tell you a story, but only to give you some advice. It is not to amuse you, but to teach you your duty. Some boys do not want to know what their duty is, for if they knew they would not do it. But I suppose you wish to know; listen then attentively to what I have written here. Your mother, or perhaps your older brother or sister, will read it to you.

Did you ever think what it is to pray? In family prayer, you all assemble in the parlour, and after reading the Bible you kneel down, and your father talks aloud; he seems to be speaking to some one; who is it that he is talking with? It is not with you – or your mother. Who is he speaking to? I once heard of a little girl whose parents were poor and bad people. They never sent her to school, not even to the Sabbath school; and she grew up a wicked girl, entirely ignorant of religion. When she was about fourteen years old she went to live in the family of a pious woman. The morning after she went to this family, just before breakfast, one of the little children came running into the kitchen, saying, 'Susan, Papa wants you to *come to prayer*.' Susan did not know what was meant by *prayer*, but knew that they wanted her to *go in;* so she followed the little boy into the parlour. The family were all seated round the room, still and quiet. The father read one of the Psalms in

Family Prayer

a serious and attentive manner; they then all kneeled down; and the father asked God to bless the whole family. Susan afterwards said, in describing this scene, that 'he talked to the wall,' and soon after asked the lady what he was talking there for so long. She did not know what it meant; but the lady explained it all to her.

Now I do not suppose you are as ignorant as Susan was; you *know* what family prayer is for, but still I know a great many children who feel and act during the morning and evening prayer of the family as they might properly do if the father was doing nothing more than talking to the wall.

I suppose you know what prayer is. It is simply asking things of God. Whether we pray secretly, or in the family, or in public, or on the Sabbath, it is simply *asking favours of God*. You very frequently ask favours of your father. In the summer you wanted a straw hat because it was hot; you asked your father for money to buy it, and he gave it you. When the winter comes, it will grow cold, and you will want a pair of mittens, and a coat, and perhaps a cap; you will ask your father for them, and if he thinks it best, he will get them for you. It is just so in prayer to God. We ask favours of Him.

JACOB ABBOTT *Religion and Happiness*

The Wicked Weed

The good lessons Margaret had learned in her younger days
at the National School, had not been forgotten by her in after-
life. She continued to practise the rules of our holy religion,
and leaned with faith and hope on the promises of the Gospel.
This made her trials comparatively light. Amidst them all,
she had a peace of mind and happiness such as the world cannot give; those persons being alone able calmly to bear the
shocks and distresses of this life who have firmly fixed their
hopes on the blessings of immortality.

In the excellent system of instruction adopted for her,
Margaret had been taught the duties of industry, cleanliness,
and regularity. These matters concerned the comfort of others,
as well as of herself, and she properly viewed them as solemn
claims upon her, which she was bound to fulfil, and which she
did fulfil to the best of her power, notwithstanding her husband's vice and improvidence. Now, whether Hubert's proposal to smoke was made in mere spite, or in utter disregard
as to what its effect must have been on her labours, it was
certainly a thing she could not help noticing, as likely to do
injury to other persons. She accordingly reminded him, that
'some of the young ladies' fine linen was laid out to be ironed;
and what would be said if, after it had been entrusted to her
to do properly, the scent of the tobacco should settle upon it?'
Who will say that this was not a fair reason? and it was
offered with the utmost tenderness of language and manner.
However, the savage fit was upon him; he could not bear being

*'He threw his pipe under
the grate, gradually drew
his chair nearer to the
family group, and listened
to the word of God'*

talked to; and grumbling something about, 'She must see to it,' lighted his pipe, then throwing himself into a chair, sat sullenly by himself.

Margaret hastily caught up the several newly-washed articles of dress; and having placed them carefully in a drawer, collected the children about her, and told the eldest boy to read a chapter in the New Testament. It was one of the many beautiful passages in the Gospel according to St. John, in which humility, mutual love, and forbearance are recommended to us by the precepts and example of Christ. As the little fellow read to the end of the thirteenth chapter, just as he would have read it at school, his father, being now somewhat sobered, overheard enough to make him heartily ashamed and sorry for his behaviour. What a temper had he shewn! how opposite to the gentleness and kindness enjoined in these words: 'A new commandment I give unto you, that ye love one another; as I have loved you that ye also love one another. By this shall all men know that ye are my disciples, if ye have love one to another.' This thought came over him in all its force: he threw his pipe under the grate, gradually drew his chair nearer to the family group, and listened to the word of God. As soon as the reading was finished, he kissed each of the children, told them to be good to their mother, and when they were gone to bed, asked Margaret's pardon for his unkindness.

ANON   *Tales and Stories*, 1847

Remember the Sabbath

A little boy was amusing himself with his playthings upon the sabbath. 'Edward,' said his mother, 'it is the sabbath day.'

'Oh, is it?' said he; 'I did not remember.'

'That is the very command which God has given us,' said his mother: "Remember the sabbath day, to keep it holy".

Children often excuse themselves by saying, 'I did not think,' 'I forgot,' 'I did not remember;' but such excuses are not acceptable to God. We may plead ignorance as an excuse for the neglect of duty, but not forgetfulness.

ANON   *Child's Companion and Juvenile Instructor*, 1861

Usefully employed

The Drunkard's Home

Several years ago, when Barnum's Museum was in Philadelphia, there was, in one of the rooms, a representation of a cold-water drinker's home, and of a drunkard's home. These were placed side by side, so as to show the contrast more strongly. The figures were all of wax, and just about the size of living persons, so that it looked very real.

The first one represented a good-sized room, with a neat carpet on the floor, and pretty paper on the walls. Two or three pictures were hanging against the sides of the room. A cheerful fire was burning in the grate. In the centre of the room stood a table with a snow-white cloth upon it. The tidy, happy-looking mother was spreading some very inviting things for breakfast; while the eldest of the children was bringing in a pitcher of water to fill the tumblers that were placed by every plate. An easy arm-chair was drawn up near the fire, and the father was leaning back in it, reading the morning paper, looking very snug and cosy in his wrapper and slippers. Around

him a group of bright-eyed, rosy-cheeked little ones were playing, while a toddling boy was tugging at his father's gown,
trying to climb up into his lap.

You did not need any one to tell you that comfort and happiness were there. Everything looked so pleasant, that one
almost felt like opening the door and walking in to share their
happiness. This was the cold-water drinker's home.

Right next to it was the other scene. It was a room with bare
floor, strewn with litter, and blackened with dirt. The plaster
was falling from the walls and the ceiling. In the fireplace there
were two or three half-burnt sticks, smouldering. An old bed-
stead stood in the corner, and a few ragged coverlets lay
tumbled in a heap upon it. The rest of the furniture consisted
of a table, and one or two rickety chairs. A loaf of bread, partly
cut, and a bottle on the table, were the only signs of a breakfast. The father, with his face unwashed, his beard unshaven,
and his hair all tangled and matted, was beating a trembling
child. The rest of the children were crowding up in the corner,
pale and frightened, but each holding on to a dry crust of
bread. Their faces were thin and sickly. The mother sat upon
the bed, her head between her hands, and her hair streaming
wildly over her shoulders. Thin and tattered rags were the only
clothes any of them had. Misery and wretchedness were as
plainly seen there, as if written with a sunbeam. This was the
drunkard's home.

Children, which is the pleasantest picture? Which would you
rather should be your home?

All the difference was made by the PITCHER and the
BOTTLE. The water in that pitcher had kept the Giant Intemperance away from the first home; while the gin in the
bottle had brought him into the other one. And it was because
HE was there, that all was so wretched. He always drives comfort and happiness out from every house he enters. He turns
gladness into sorrow, smiles into sighs, laughter into tears,
wherever he goes. He makes his prisoners miserable themselves,
and all about them unhappy too. Mothers and fathers, wives
and children, brothers and sisters, suffer wherever he comes.

RICHARD NEWTON
The Giants and How to Fight Them, 1875

32

The Evening Meal

The humblest cottager wears a smile during the happy season of harvest. Every one that is of age to work, is then fully employed, and well paid. Money comes in freely, and the pinch of want is not felt as at other times in the dwellings of the poor. At the first gleam of early sunshine, the industrious peasant, with such of his sons as are able to assist in his labours, goes forth, carrying in his scrip, or bag, a portion of food sufficient for the day. At eight o'clock, his careful wife, after giving her family their breakfast, leads out her little train to glean, leaving her eldest girl to keep house, nurse the babe, and take care of any of the children who are too young to glean. She has also to scrub or sweep the floor, and cook the supper against the return of the family. The supper, which is always the principal meal, generally consists of hard flour-dumplings, with vegetables, and sometimes, as in harvest-time, a morsel of meat, and a drop of gravy by way of sauce. I am always delighted, when returning from my evening walks, to peep into the cottages of the Suffolk peasants, and see the various members of families, that have been dispersed in laborious vocations all day, collecting in smiling groups round a cleanly but humble board, and enjoying the pleasure of an affectionate re-union at the evening meal. On one occasion, I observed a table neatly spread outside the cottage door, and the good man and his family supping in the open air, under the loaded branches of a fine apple tree. Believe me, Caroline, it was a pretty sight to see the parents feeding their little ones, and the eldest girl, a careful little house-wife, of twelve years old, with a smiling countenance, waiting upon the whole party. I have sketched the group for your Album, but can scarcely hope that you will be as well pleased with the shadow, as I was with the reality of the scene.

AGNES STRICKLAND and BERNARD BARTON
Fisher's Juvenile Scrapbook, 1837

Sulky Tom

The Evil Influence of Uncle Murray

Poor Anna was in this dangerous state, when, one day while she was in the drawing-room, her Aunt Ross received a letter, which seemed to displease her very much. After reading it more than once, she threw it on the table, saying 'How provoking! I had quite forgotten that tiresome, vulgar uncle!' Then turning to Anna, she said, 'Here is a letter from your Uncle Murray, my dear, to remind me, as he says, that the six months you were to spend with us is now elapsed, and that he will be here himself in two days to take you home with him for the next six months. I am quite vexed at this,' continued Aunt Ross, looking very much displeased. 'You will lose every thing you have got. I have done all I could to improve you. Your uncle has determined to add to your fortune, so as to make it equal to Louisa's. You are two of the most elegant little girls to be seen – every one says so; and to take you away to live at a Scotch minister's! Vulgar people, without fortune, or any advantage; and to associate with their rude hobbish boys. How could your parents make such a will!'

'Mamma loved Uncle Murray,' said Anna, who never could bear to hear any reflection thrown on her own Mamma. 'Well, well,' replied Aunt Ross, 'your Mamma had some strange notions; but what is to be done now? I would not for the world you should lose all the advantages you have got with me; and six months is such a time at your age. All the other little girls will get before you, and Louisa never attended to any thing half so well till you came. What shall I do?' Aunt Ross thought for a little, then said, joyfully, 'Ah! that will do! Miss Palmer shall go with you; and I can get another governess for Louisa, whom I can myself superintend; and her French governess is to be with us immediately. That will do delightfully, and as much as possible counteract the evil you would acquire at your uncle's. Poor Miss Palmer, to be sure, will not like to bury herself in such a place; but your uncle will increase her salary for the time. You may go to the school-room, my dears, for I must settle all this immediately.' So Aunt Ross rung the bell, and desired the servant to tell a lie, and say she was not at home, though she was; and the children went off to the school-room.

GRACE KENNEDY *Anna Ross*, 1848

Right: Title Page. *Peter Parley's Annual* appeared from 1840 to 1888

34

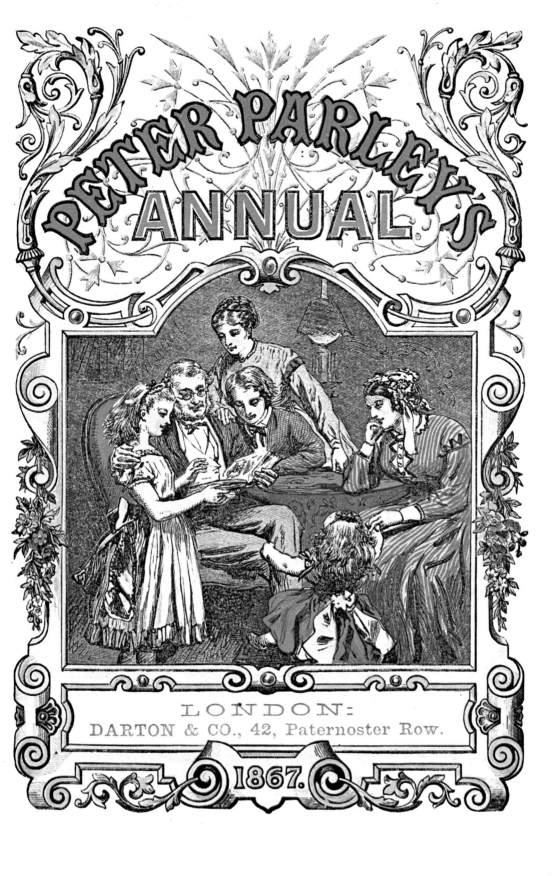

PETER PARLEY'S ANNUAL

LONDON:
DARTON & CO., 42, Paternoster Row.

1867.

The Model Lodging House

Two years passed quietly away, and Nancy Godwin became the wife of Harry Bryant. The London home to which he had brought her was in the outskirts of the great city. It consisted of two rooms on the first floor of a small house in a long street. There was no garden, but a small court-yard in the rear, in which stood a small washhouse, a dust-bin, and a water-butt. Besides the Bryants there were two other couples living in the house, both of whom had young children; and the landlady who kept it lived on the basement floor, in the general kitchen, of which all the lodgers had the use. Bryant had furnished his rooms well and substantially, and indeed had spared no necessary expense; so that Nancy was delighted when she found herself so rich in household goods. Those first summer months were a sort of fairy season to the youthful pair.

But before long there came a change. With the fall of the year came wet weather for days together. The new home, which at first had looked so bright, began to lose some of its charms. November brought its fogs, which seemed to settle in that low region as though they would never depart. Nancy took cold, and had to nurse herself, and Bryant was full of fears on her account.

He had eaten his dinner in the workshop one day, and was sitting by the stove in a rather thoughtful mood, when his eye fell upon a printed paper which one of the men had left on his bench. Bryant took it up listlessly, and began to read. It was a description of some new houses, called Model Lodging-houses, which had lately been opened in the neighbourhood for the accommodation of working men and their families. He had not time to read the whole then, but he borrowed the

paper of his comrade, and put it in his pocket. At night he took it home, and he and Nancy read it together. There they found that, for a less sum than they were then paying, they could have two good rooms in a large, healthy house, with a constant supply of water, cold or hot, the use of a bath, a washhouse, a large drying-room, a kitchen fire for cooking, with many other conveniences of which they were now deprived, and that, in addition to all, there was a room set apart for reading, and supplied with books and newspapers. 'Nancy,' said Bryant, 'do you put on your cloak to-morrow morning, as soon as you have had your breakfast, and go and see what this is like; you will be able to judge better than I can. If it suits your taste it will be sure to suit mine, and we will move our sticks there at once. It is not ten minutes' walk from our shop, so that I can pop in and out for dinner, and even for tea, if I like.'

Nancy was too well pleased at the thought of escaping from her present lodging to lose time in doing as she was requested. By ten o'clock next morning she was in the new lodging-house, and being shown over it by the director. She found everything exactly as it was described in the paper she had read. Before leaving, the porter put into her hand a paper of the regulations to be observed by all the inmates. On reaching home she felt so pleased with what she had seen that she could not help mentioning it to Mrs Pain, the mother of some noisy children in the top floor.

'Oh,' said Mrs Pain, 'I know all about them Model Lodging-houses; one may as well go into a prison at once as go there.'

'Why so?' said Nancy, rather alarmed.

'Why, you see, it's just as strict as a prison. You just look at the regulations, and you'll see.'

'I have looked at them,' said Nancy, 'and really I see nothing to complain of;' and she took them from her pocket.

'Don't you? then I do. Why, you've got to sweep other people's dirt as well as your own. Look there!' and she pointed to the rule.

'But that is only in your turn,' said Nancy; 'and surely it is better that one person should do the whole in her turn, than that twenty should be sweeping at once.'

'Oh, but you can't stay out after eleven o'clock without a ticket; and my husband wouldn't stand that, I know, if yours would. Then you must pay your rent aforehand every Monday morning; and if you don't be sharp with it, out you go. And there's other things besides as isn't to my taste, I can tell you.'

This conversation was rather a damper to Nancy; but when Bryant came home she gave him a faithful account of all, not forgetting Mrs Pain's objections. It was resolved to give the Model Lodging-house a trial, in spite of Mrs Pain. On the following day Bryant called at the place himself, and hired two nice rooms, and before the week had expired they had moved into them. There was an end at once to the water difficulty; there was quiet in the rooms, for the walls were too thick for common sounds to pass through; there were the means of cleanliness always at hand, in baths for the person, and washing and drying rooms for linen; and at all times of the day there was the kitchen fire for cooking. As for the regulations which frightened Mrs Pain, a little experience showed that they were the best that could have been devised for the comfort of the inmates, who were insured by them the enjoyment of peace, cleanliness, and order. Both Bryant and his wife had their health in their new home, where, in course of time, they formed many agreeable acquaintances among an honest and frugal class, whose intimacy was of use to them in after-life.

ANON   *The Cottage at the Firs*

Saturday Night

It was worth while to notice the conduct of some of the labourers' wives just about pay-time. Some of them looked merry and cheerful as larks, had made themselves as neat as a new pin, and having finished all the household work of the week, had cleaned up their cottages and got everything in Sunday order long before Saturday's sun had set. With others it was quite different. They hardly had the means of making themselves neat, and they had lost heart so much that they did not care about making the best of what they had. You would see these poor women, about the time the wages were paid, leaving their cottages, and perhaps dragging a child or two along with them, and making haste to the public-house, where they would stand sometimes for hours, to catch their husbands before they went in, in order to get as much of the wages out of their hands as they could before it was wasted in drink. A sad sight that is!

If you had looked in at Godwin's cottage about that time, you would have seen it in capital trim, a bright little fire burning in the grate, the kettle singing on the hob, and father's cup and saucer on the table waiting for him to sit down to tea. John comes as punctual as the clock, and when he has had his tea, he and Mary, or he and Nancy if his wife is busy, take the market-basket and set off to buy the necessary provisions for the following week: flour for their bread, which Mary makes herself, a pound or two of butcher's meat for Sunday's dinner, tea, sugar, and whatever happens to be wanted. John had paid his club-money on his way home, and if he had anything to

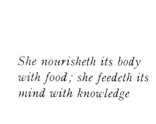

She nourisheth its body with food; she feedeth its mind with knowledge

spare he has made a small deposit in the savings bank as well; so that he knows what he has to spend, and knows, too, how to make the most of it. There is no market in Newton, as there is in large towns, where housekeepers can go and choose at a hundred stalls or more, and suit their fancy just as they like. Instead of an open market, there is only the general shop kept by Mrs Mold; and if she has not got the thing you want, it is likely you may have to do without it. But Mrs Mold knows the wants of her customers pretty well, and, to-say the truth, she has got everything they are likely to ask for, and a good many things which you and I might imagine would never be called for. She has butchers' meat and dried fish, groceries of all kinds, faggots and firewood, bales of calico and bright-printed dresses, flitches of bacon, fruit and vegetables, and fustian jackets, smock-frocks, and hats and caps, and no end of earthen pots and pans and crockery-ware, to say nothing of knives and forks, and spoons, and flat-irons, and frying-pans, and all manner of domestic hardware. So, you see, the general shop does not make a bad market for a poor man, or a poor man's wife, who is pretty sure to find what she wants there

ANON   *The Cottage at the Firs*

Little Fred

When little Fred went to bed,
He always said his prayers.
He kissed mamma and then papa,
And straightway went upstairs.

ANON   *The National Nursery Book*

Sunday Afternoons with Mamma

Sunday was a happy day to little Kate and Ernest. Shall I tell you how they spent it? On Saturday evening, just before bed-time, they always helped their nurse to put away in the nursery cupboard all their toys and their 'week day' Picture Books, and then from a drawer below was taken, first a box of moveable letters, which Kate and Ernest (or Erny as he was usually called) were only allowed to use on Sunday.

The children were very fond of putting these letters together so as to form words, and they often were able to spell a verse from the Bible in this way.

But besides the letter box, in the Sunday drawer were kept two large Picture Books, with large coloured pictures of Bible scenes. One of these belonged to Katie, and the other to Erny, and there were some smaller books as well, with pretty Bible stories, and sweet hymns in them. All these were taken out of the drawer on Saturday night, and put away again on Sunday night, because if Katie and Erny had had these letters and books every day, they would, perhaps, have grown tired of them, and would have had no fresh books for Sunday.

Then dear mamma always tried to make Sunday a very happy day to her children; and when they were not happy, I think it must have been either when they were not very well, or not very good.

In the morning they went to the house of God with their papa and mamma, and although they could not know all that was said, yet they tried to behave well, that they might not disturb other people. The good minister sometimes spoke to the children who were present, and then they tried not to forget what he said, that they might tell mamma about it by-and-by. And when all the people knelt in prayer, their mamma had told them that they could think a little prayer in their heart, and that, though they did not speak, God would hear what their hearts said to him.

Katie and Erny always liked to hear the singing; sometimes they almost knew the hymns and tunes, from hearing them sung very often, and then they were able to help sing God's praises with their young voices.

On Sundays they had the pleasure of dining and taking tea with papa and mamma, instead of in the nursery, as on other days; and though they were very fond of nurse, and quite happy with her, this was a great treat.

But it is about their Sunday afternoons with mamma that I

Bible studies

am going to tell you. Katie and Erny spent them alone with
her. Nurse and all the other servants but one, went to worship
God, and papa went to the ragged school, to teach some poor
little boys who had not any kind fathers or mothers at home
to tell them how the Lord Jesus loves little children.

Sometimes Katie and Erny read to their mamma from one of
their Sunday story books. Then she read to them, and they
learned a short text, or one or two verses of a hymn. But what
they best liked, was listening to the stories their mamma told
them from the Bible.

When papa came home, he often had something to say about
the poor little ragged boys in his class. I believe Katie and
Erny knew almost all their names, although they had only seen
one or two of them, and they often asked a great many
questions about them at tea-time.

After tea, papa was glad to rest a little, and then mamma
opened the piano, and played and sang with her children some
sweet children's hymns. They almost always finished with the
one beginning:

Jesus, tender Shepherd, hear me,
Bless thy little lamb to-night,
Through the darkness be thou near me,
Keep me safe till morning light.

Then nurse came to call the children to the nursery, and after a happy talk with her, and kneeling down and thanking God for all his love and care during the day, and asking him to watch them through the night, Kate and Ernest were almost always ready for bed, and soon might be seen fast asleep on their little pillows.

ANON   *Sunday Afternoons with Mamma*

Cottager's Sunday

Many of our readers who pass their lives amidst quiet rural scenes, must often have noticed how peacefully the Sunday morning dawns upon a retired village. There is no jingling and rattling of chains and harness, no trampling of horses, and grinding of wheels in the ruts of the road, no hammering at the blacksmith's forge, no sound of mower whetting his scythe, or reaper grinding his sickle; but all is calm and still. Early on the summer morning, the slender wreaths of smoke, first from one cottage chimney and then from another, begin to curl upwards among the dark green trees; the casements are thrown open; then the door swings upon its hinges, and a smiling face or two looks out upon the welcome sunshine. Then husbands and fathers come forth with leisurely step, lingering among their plots of flowers, and kindly greetings and inquiries are exchanged among friends and neighbours. Then follows the frugal morning meal, the only breakfast in the week at which the labourer sees all his family around him; then, let us hope, the chapter in the Bible is read, and while all kneel around the board, thanksgivings are offered to the Father of all mercies, and a blessing is asked on the privileges and services of the day.

At least this is the way in which Sunday begins in John Godwin's cottage. And breakfast has not been very long over, when, from many a cottage-door, children of all ages, and in groups of various numbers, are seen with polished faces, and clean and tidily clad, hastening towards the open door of the Sunday-school in the rear of the old square-towered, ivy-covered church. All four of the young Godwins go regularly to the Sunday-school; for though Nancy is over fifteen, and Sam is but a year younger, their parents see no reason why they should quit the school, where they are taught to know the Bible, and to make it the rule of their actions, that they may be the better able to encounter the snares and temptations of the world. Indeed, Nancy's parents have resolved that she shall attend the Sunday-school until she quits them to go out to service, as she is looking forward to do when she is old enough.

Just at ten o'clock, that one little bell in the ivy-clad tower of the old church, which can be plainly seen through the wide stone bars of the window, begins wagging backwards and for-wards with a rather clanking sound, to call the villagers to worship. As it tolls for half an hour, it does not seem to excite much attention at first, though no doubt many a busy dame bestirs herself at its first note, in order not to be behind time. But before long the broad, winding street of the village begins to show signs of life. At first a few grey-haired men, bowed with age, attended by wives as old and decrepit, or stayed on the arms of sturdy son or loving daughter, take their slow and deliberate way. Among them is seen the cripple on his crutches, or perhaps the sick man who has lately risen from his bed of pain, whom the fine morning has tempted forth, that he may return thanks for his recovery in the house of God. The strong and healthy come after – labouring men in snow-white smock-frocks, thrifty housewives in trim printed gowns, matronly dames in bright scarlet cloaks, elder sisters in charge of chubby-faced little ones; and you notice that not a few of the church-goers carry splendid flowers in their button-holes or their bosoms – the very pride of their gardens, which they have reserved for Sunday morning wear. As the crowd are nearing the avenue which leads to the churchyard, up drives the squire's carriage, with the squire and his lady in it, while all stand aside to let it pass. Then there is Farmer Fowler's trap, full of blooming boys and girls; and after them come a few stragglers from more distant places. There is some pausing in the avenue, and greetings under the trees from neighbours who live far apart and meet but rarely; but when the little bell peals double time, denoting that it will stop in three minutes, there is a general move for the open church door, and in a moment more all have entered.

ANON   *The Cottage at the Firs*

The Father's Return

All the day long, in the cornfield so weary,
Father has toiled in the heat of the sun;
Now the great bell from the farm-yard rings cheery
Telling the time of his labour is done.

A Sunday at the Fairchilds

On the Sunday morning, the family generally rose a little earlier than usual, in order that everything which was necessary might be finished before breakfast – such things, I mean, as feeding the pigs, milking the cow, getting parsley for the hare, and giving corn to the fowls and pigeons. The children were always allowed bread and butter and tea for breakfast on a Sunday. And after breakfast all the family made haste to dress themselves; and having made up the fire and locked the doors, they used to set off to the village; for the school and the church were in the village. Many pleasant walks had Mr Fairchild and his family, on a summer's morning to the village church; Henry, Lucy, and Emily walked quietly first (for they were not allowed to run on a Sunday), Mr and Mrs Fairchild coming up next, and Betty and John behind. Mrs Baker's neat little house was just at the entrance of the village, the very first house after John Trueman's; and unless something very particular happened, Mrs Baker was always ready to come out, and go with Mrs Fairchild to school.

When they came to the schools, Mr Fairchild and Henry went to the boys' school, and Mrs Fairchild and her little girls, with Mrs Baker, went into the girls' school; there they heard the children their Catechism, and heard them read, and gave them religious instruction. Lucy and Emily had each six little girls less than themselves, and Henry as many little boys to hear. They generally contrived to be two hours at school, before it was time to go to church. When they knew, by the church bell, that it was time to leave the schools, the children were all placed two and two, and taken to church. Henry walked by his little boys, and sat with them at church, to find their Psalters, and to see that they behaved well; and Emily and Lucy kept by their little girls for the same purpose.

After the Divine Service was over, Mr and Mrs Fairchild and their family came home; and the children, if they pleased, had a bit of bread as soon as they came in. But there was one thing which Mr Fairchild would not allow his family to do – a thing which many people are very much in the practice of – that is, when they have been at church, hearing the good word of God, to come home and chatter together about foolish things, till they have quite forgotten all the holy words they have heard in the church. 'You might just as well,' Mr Fairchild would say, 'sow good seeds in your fields, and then turn in a flock of birds to pick them all up, as go to church, and

afterwards meet, and talk, and chatter, till you have forgotten
everything you have heard.' So Mrs Fairchild ordered her
children, when they came in from church, whilst they were
waiting for their dinner, to go each one into a place apart by
themselves, where they might think of what they had been
hearing. Sometimes they would walk alone in the garden, or
in a path which was in a coppice just by, if it was a fine day;
or go into their own little rooms to pray, and sing a hymn, and
think of God. Henry, in particular, had a little favourite shady
path in the coppice, where scarcely ever any person came,
excepting two old women, whose cottages were on that side
of the coppice; and there you might see him walking up and
down, praying, or singing his hymns, till he was called to
dinner by the dinner-bell, which John always rang out of the
house door.

At dinner Mr Fairchild would not allow his family to speak of
the business of the week days, nor even to talk of their neighbours: they found enough of pleasant discourse in speaking of
what they had heard in the church, or of what had happened
in the school; which of the children were improved, and who
said the Catechism best, and who got rewards, and such things.
After dinner, in the long days, they all went again to church;
but in the winter they could not go in the evening, because
there was no service. So when they could not go to church,
Mr Fairchild was the clergyman, and Henry the clerk; and
Mrs Fairchild, and Lucy and Emily, and John and Betty, and
the two old women who lived in the coppice, who generally
drank tea with Betty on a Sunday evening, made up the congregation. After Evening Service came tea; and when tea was
over, the children were allowed to read any pretty Sunday
book they had; and amongst them they had a great many.
Before they went to bed, Mr Fairchild heard them read a few
chapters in the Bible, and repeat the Church Catechism. Then
they all sang some hymns together, and prayed; and when they
had had their baked apples (or, if it was summer time, perhaps
some strawberries and cream, or raspberries and cream), the
children went to bed.

MRS SHERWOOD *The History of the Fairchild Family*,
1880 Edition

Beware of the Fire

Beware of the fire! beware of the fire!
I can't have you playing so near –
You really must learn to be careful, my pets,
Or mischief will happen, I fear.

I know the guard's up, but then just as I spoke,
I saw a hot coal drop below,
And children don't watch when they're frisking about,
Where skirts, string, and pinafores go.

Remember Kate Morris – poor, dear little girl –
So merry, so active and bright;
So happy and full of gay spirits one morn,
A scorched, blackened corpse the same night . . .

ANON The Children's Friend, May 1865

Our Queen

You cannot know and feel the full meaning of 'God save the
Queen' until you are acquainted with the history of your
country and its other kings and queens; and after that it will
do you good to read about other countries, and compare them.
If any little boy or girl wants to know how he or she ought to
feel when singing 'God save the Queen,' I can only indicate
the 'how,' by saying, sing it as if the words were 'God save
Mamma,' and then you will sing it with heart and voice. Our
Queen Victoria has always shown herself a good mother to
her own children (who had also a good father), and full of

"GOD SAVE OUR GRACIOUS QUEEN."

'Sing it as if the words were "God save Mamma"' kindness and *motherliness* towards her people. She has always encouraged the best men to help in the government of the country, has never hesitated about giving her consent to new laws that were shown to be easier and better than the old ones, and has always held herself aloof from that old fashioned habit of heaping up favours upon heads that have done nothing to merit them. The more you try to find out about OUR QUEEN the more heartily will you sing GOD BLESS HER.

ANON   *The Children's Pleasure Book,* 1874

Papa's Blessing

A party of friends were one evening assembled round the table at a meal, and, after some little time, two children, who were present, were observed to sit looking at their food, while all the others were going forward. 'Why do you not proceed, my dear?' asked a lady.

'Because papa has not asked a blessing,' replied the infant voices.

ANON   *The Children's Friend*, February 1868

POVERTY & RICHES

The Factories Acts after 1832 showed that the State was beginning to intervene in the problems of poverty and Exploitation during the Industrial Revolution. The parishes, or Unions of parishes, were responsible for the destitute in the workhouses, under the Guardians of the Poor. When official 'outdoor relief' came to an end, bringing charity to the poor in their own homes became the province of the privileged.

Juvenile writers were at pains to point out to budding charity workers that God, and not economics or the greed of the mercantile class, was responsible for the sorting out of the haves and the have nots. All the same, children were urged to make their little contributions towards an improvement on the Divine order of things. Comforts, the Word, and Education, it seemed, would bring about an ideal situation.

Nobody thought of suggesting that the rich would then be indistinguishable from the poor. This would have undermined the moral purpose: to arouse compassion, to nourish a sense of thrift and a habit of sensible giving. Spontaneous generosity was frowned on. Perhaps it suggested irrational extravagance. To a child trained in Evangelism, 'Love Thy Neighbour' did not mean treat him as an equal. Nor was 'Brotherhood' interpreted as social justice. The poor were a category to be saved, not individuals to be civilised and transformed. The rich had not thought yet of bringing their own culture to the poor by benevolent picnicking in Settlements. The Salvation Army (founded in 1865), recruited from the class it was meant to be saving, met the challenge on an equal, and rollicking, footing.

To prove that good behaviour – in other words, happiness – did not depend on financial security, the responsible poor were shown to have middle-class values. They were devout, diligent and well-mannered. But the irresponsible were, of course, unhappy. They were naughty. That is, they did not put economic considerations first, they were slothful and therefore ignorant, and above all they did not fear God.

Never Waste *Anything*

While some poor children that I meet
Have very little food to eat,
Thanks to my heavenly Father's care,
I have enough, and some to spare.

Then never must I waste that bread,
By which the hungry may be fed,
For those who throw their food away,
May live to want that food some day.

Not anything should I destroy,
Which others may for good employ;
Nor even tread beneath my feet
A crumb some little bird would eat.

I must not little things despise,
For much from little things may rise;
And every moment, every mite,
Is of some worth when used aright.

ANON *Choice Poetry for Little Children*

To stroll about and
drink her gin,
She loves far better
than to spin,
Or work to earn her
bread

Children of the Poor

And is it not a pity that those poor children, who are now so happy and so innocent, will, for want of that education which you are favoured with, and for that watchful care which your fond parents keep over you, be left to wander about wherever they choose; untaught and uncared for, will many of them run from street to street with Lucifer-matches to sell, or from door to door begging a mouthful of bread; or mingle with other children, who through bad examples have fallen into evil ways; who never had a fond mother to kneel down before while they said their prayers, ere they retired to sleep, or a kind father to take them in his arms and bless·them when they arose in the morning. Oh! you would shudder if you could but trace the future career of many of those poor children whom you see on a warm Spring evening so playful and happy, in spite of all their dirt and rags, as they emerge from the courts and alleys where they have been shut up all the winter long. I know I am writing to warm-hearted English boys, possessed of noble feelings, and I am sure that when they pass these poor neglected children they will feel sorry for them; and that if ever they possess the power in after-life, they will lend their aid in establishing schools, and endeavouring to alleviate the misery which hangs about those wretched courts and alleys, and such kind actions will bring their own reward.

THOMAS MILLER *The Boy's Spring Book*, 1847

Charity Elicited

Fanny, who knew all about Gravesend, as it was the nearest large town to Fairdown, explained to Arthur that all these people did not live at Gravesend, but that most of them were people from London, who came out with their families for a day's pleasure in the fresh air on the river, and to walk about Gravesend. Fanny said that many working-men and quite poor people were able to do this once or twice in the summer, because the fare on the steam-boats was so little. Arthur was very glad to hear this, because he had often pitied the poor pale, dirty children, whom he saw playing in the London streets, and wished they could go to the sea-side and into the country, sometimes as he and his sisters and brothers did. He now

*his poor creature in
the picture . . .
azes in the faces of
the passengers, not
liking to ask alms*

watched the children in the crowd very earnestly, and felt
very glad to see how pleased and joyful they looked.

'I wish I were a king,' he exclaimed at length, 'I would give
every poor family money enough to come down here every
week.'

'Yes,' said Fanny, 'and if I were a queen, they should all
have nice dinners every day, and plenty of clothes to wear,
and clean houses to live in.'

'I suppose they all have nice dinners to-day, Fanny. I mean,
all these people. That little boy looks hungry, though – the
one looking into the cake shop, I think I will give him sixpence out of my half-crown; shall I, Fanny?'

'Yes, dear, he does look hungry. James,' said she to the

man on the box, 'will you let me hold the reins while you get change for Arthur's half-crown?' Now, James had heard what the children had been saying, and was very pleased that they thought of other people who were not so well off as themselves, and he. knew that Fanny could hold the reins properly, because he had taught her before, and that the horses were very steady and would stand; so he said 'Yes, Missy, I can give Master Arthur change; but that poor boy wants meat and not cakes, and I will just run across to that eating-house with him, and get him a slice of hot meat and some potatoes and bread, for sixpence.'

'Oh thank you, thank you, James,' said Arthur. James gave Fanny the reins, and she held them well while he ran across with the poor boy and took him into the eating-house. In another minute, James was back on the box again, and told them that the poor boy was very much obliged to them.

MISS WINNARD   *Fanny and Arthur*

Pity the Poor City Arabs

A Halfpenny for poor Milo

. . . They never gather'd weeds or shells
Among the shining sand,
Nor shouted as the bright sea-waves
Came bounding to the land.

They only knew the courts and lanes
Where seldom shone the sun,
Where all was wretchedness and rags
And cruel deeds were done.

Where gin and beer-shops opened wide
Their doors of shame and sin,
Where men and women slew themselves
With beer and fiery gin.

They heard the words the drunkard's spoke,
Too horrible to tell,
And, mingled with these awful words,
The drunkard's shriek and yell.

Pity the Poor City Arabs

So these poor children, when night came,
Were glad to seek repose
Far from the public-house's din,
The drunkard's shrieks and blows.

And now these homeless little boys,
In the cold archway sleep:
Poor children! when the morning comes
They will awake to weep.

Oh, children, in your happy homes,
Pity these children poor,
Who have no friends, no home, and who
Such misery endure.

In prayer remember them each day,
And give what you can spare;
In all your comforts and your joys
Oh, let them have some share.

Remember the great God who made
The world and then made you;
The Saviour, who for you hath died,
Died for these children too.

Be friends unto these friendless ones,
Help them in their sore need;
And in their heartfelt gratitude
You will be bless'd indeed.

R.P.S.

NOTE *Our readers can help the poor lads of London by sub-
scribing to the Ragged School Union, Exeter Hall, Strand; or
the National Temperance League, 337, Strand, London. Both
these Societies are working most actively in reclaiming and
helping the children of the poor outcasts.*
ANON *The Children's Friend*, November 1868

White Mice

Was I a Good Boy?

'Mamma, I gave a penny to a poor man this morning. Was I a good boy for so doing?' 'It depends upon the motive you had in view. Did you give it him because you thought he was poor? or because you thought I should call you a good boy?' 'Because I thought you would call me a good boy, mamma.' 'I am sorry to hear it, my dear; tell me just what you thought when you gave the penny to the man.' 'Well, mamma, I saw him coming up the garden, and when he knocked at the door I went to him, and he asked for a morsel of bread. So I just thought of a penny I had in my pocket, and I said to myself, "Now if I give this penny, mamma will call me a good boy, and then I shall be glad:" and so I gave it him.' 'Now, my dear, this is what you should have said: – "This old man is very poor, and I have a penny to spare, that will do him good, and he shall have it."' 'Ah! mamma, I wish I had thought of that but I am sure I did not intend to do wrong! you know, mamma, I love you so dearly that I strive to please you in all things.' 'Yes, my dear, I know you love me, and I believe you did not intend to do wrong; but, my dear child, we are so apt to act as that we may be praised of men, instead of doing all things to the glory of God. Do you not know, my love, that our Lord said in his sermon on the mount, "Take heed that ye do not your alms before men, to be seen of them: otherwise ye have no reward of your Father, which is in heaven!" You will try to think of this, will you, love?' 'Oh! dearest mamma, I am sure I will, and I hope that God
Will grant me pardon for the past,
And strength for time to come.'

MRS JERRAM *Child's Own Story Book*, 1840

Little Ellen

Mr Grey was not a rich man, but he always found the means to relieve those who were poorer than himself, and in all his acts of benevolence he found a ready assistant in his amiable and affectionate wife, who was willing to make any sacrifice and to take any trouble for the relief of the poor villagers. Little Ellen was early trained to assist in these acts of mercy; nothing could give her greater pleasure than to accompany

A friend in need

her dear parents on their walks through the village. How lightly would she trip before them, her basket laden with delicacies which the poor sick people could not procure for themselves; she always reached the cottager's door before her good parents, and oh! how gentle was the tap she gave – not a boisterous knock, but a gentle tap, tap, tap; for though Ellen had good spirits herself, she remembered that the sick are often very much depressed, and cannot bear the slightest noise; then when the door was opened, she would steal gently up to the bedside, her lovely little face glowing with pleasure, softened by pity, and say, 'Here, dame, I have brought you some strawberries; they are the first from my own strawberry bed, and I asked John to gather them for you; these roses too I thought they would make your room more cheerful; papa and mamma are coming down the lane, but I reached here before them.' How grateful were the poor people for these little acts of kindness, and how often was Ellen requited with the words,

Poverty and Riches

'God bless you and reward you, dear Miss Ellen.' She always accompanied her dear mamma in her visits to the village school, and when Miss Ellen made her appearance, the eyes of the poor little children glistened with delight, for Ellen showed no pride because she was the vicar's daughter, but always had some kind word to say to each of them.

ANN THORP   *Aunt Kate's Story*, 1846

Where is his supper?

Some Have No Home

I pity those who have no home,
But beg their bread, or idly roam:
Some young as I, no mother's care,
Nor father's tender kindness share.

Like them, without a home and wild,
I might have been a beggar's child,
The pains of hunger oft to feel,
And learn, like some of them, to steal.

I pity them, and if I could,
How I should like to do them good;
To tell them of the Saviour's love,
And of a better world above.

That world of joy, that home of peace,
Where love shall never, never cease;
Where there is room for all to meet,
Before our heavenly Father's feet.

ANON *Choice Poems for Little Children*

Blessed are They... but why?

Not that there was much to be seen. Only a few carts and one or two carriages passing now and then, or a foot-passenger hurrying on, as if anxious to reach home quickly. Presently a lamplighter came briskly along, bearing his ladder; for though not yet dark, the afternoon had begun to draw in. It was quite a respectable thoroughfare – this cross-road at the end of the little alley. Kitty would have liked to walk in it, but she seldom ventured there alone. It was too much the region of well-dressed people and policemen.

Suddenly a gleam of something white on the pavement attracted her eye. She stepped forward and picked it up with her little dusky hand. Only a piece of paper, torn on two sides, with words printed on it in very large letters. Kitty was not much of a reader, but she had learned a little; and stealing a few steps nearer to a lamp, she tried to make it out – slowly, and spelling each syllable. They were strange words. Kitty could hardly believe her own eyesight.

'Blessed are they which do hunger and thirst.'

Nothing more than that. What could it mean? Blessed to be hungry and thirsty! If it had been, 'Blessed are they which do *not* hunger and thirst,' Kitty would have agreed most heartily. She spelt it over a second time, to be quite sure there was no mistake. But no! – there were the words as plainly as they could be printed. Folding up the paper, she bestowed it in a safe corner of her ragged dress, and leaned against the corner house to think.

Kitty was very much perplexed. She was not quite ignorant of the meaning of the word 'blessed.' No doubt, if she had been asked to explain it, she would have given but a misty and uncertain answer. Still she knew that it meant something good – something nice – something to be desired. And how could it be either good, or nice, or desirable to be hungry and thirsty?

Kitty did not think that it was. She felt quite sure that the author of those words could never have known real hunger – sharp, gnawing, pinching hunger, such as she felt at that moment. She had had nothing to eat since early morning, and nothing then but a crust of bread. She would have given a great deal, if she had had it, for another crust, however small. And this bit of paper seemed to make out that it was *good* to feel as she did then – that she would not be really any better off if she had plenty to eat and drink.

'Oh yes, we'll work like honest boys,
And if our mother should look down,
She'd like to see us with a broom,
And with a crossing of our own.'
From *Mother's Last Words* (see page **209**)

'Then ladies, dear ladies, your pity bestow.'
A touching scene from *The Poll Parrot Picture Book*

'No one could think it nice and pleasant to be hungry and thirsty, if there was nothing to eat or drink'

No, Kitty could not agree to the little sentence. And yet she could not help believing, even while unable to understand it. The words seemed to sink down deep into her mind, and remain there. She would like to be blessed, she thought. Was it possible that being hungry and thirsty could make her so? And what, after all, was the real meaning of *blessed?* It must be something more than she knew. No one could think of nice and pleasant to be hungry or thirsty, if there was nothing to eat or drink. It was very puzzling.

ANON   *Hungering and Thirsting*

Let England help...

Through the kindness of a benevolent lady, who has travelled extensively in America and in various parts of the world, we have pleasure in giving our readers a picture of one of the rooms in the Coloured Orphan Asylum in New York. This lady writes – 'I have visited the asylum, and never saw one more admirably conducted, or the children better trained.' Our object in calling the attention of our young friends to this subject, is, that we may enlist their sympathy, prayer, and help, on behalf of the *eight hundred thousand* black children who, with their parents, have recently been liberated from slavery in the Southern States of America. At present these poor children are enduring fearful sufferings, from the want of food and clothes.

Until the death-blow was struck to the horrid system of slavery, it was a *crime* to teach any slave to read or write. Now that the slaves have become freed men, they are most anxious to learn to read. The eagerness with which some of the poor old negroes are now striving to learn to read the Bible is most remarkable.

There are now about four millions of freedmen in America, and unless they are supplied with warm clothing during this winter, it is feared that tens of thousands of them will perish from starvation.

Many English ladies and little girls, are actively at work making clothes for these poor coloured people. From the City of Bristol, about 5,000 garments have been sent. It is hoped that if the poor blacks are helped through this winter, many of them will, next year, be able to get work and support themselves.

In the mean time let England *help* these long-oppressed ones in their passage from bondage to sudden liberty.

ANON   *The Children's Friend*, 1865

The Poor Rustic

Harvest Home is the great August festival in the country. It used to be a day of good fellowship between the employer and the employed – between the worthy old English farmer and his husbandmen, whom he then looked upon as belonging to his own family; and the well-fed and decently-clothed – looked up to him as their father. Now alas! all is changed.

The farmer has lost his fine old humanity, and screws down the poor labourer to the most miserable pittance, and he is, literally, half-starved. Eight shillings a week to support a wife and family! Think of this, you black-emancipating Englishwomen! Just look a little into our English cottager's dwelling. See the poor rustic, after a hard day's labour in the ploughed field, coming home, hungry and exhausted, with nothing to eat but a few cold potatoes and a bit of bread and cheese. Think of him coming off the frozen stubbles in the winter to a miserable modicum of fire, not sufficient to warm his toes, and going to bed at six o'clock to save fire and candle – to his bed of chaff – his rude palette – his one little room, perhaps, in which six or seven people are crowded for the benefit of 'typhus.' – Think of this, and a great deal more than I could describe, ye philosophers of the Philadelphian!

But the Harvest! Among the heathens, the masters of families, when they had got in their harvest, were wont to feast with their servants who had laboured with them in tilling the ground. In strict conformity with this, it is common among the people calling themselves Christians, when the fruits of the earth are gathered and laid in their proper repositories, to provide a plentiful supper for the harvestmen and the servants of the family. In old times, there was no distinction of persons, but master and servant sat together at the same table, conversed freely together, and spent the remainder of the night in dancing, and singing innocent songs. Festivity is the reflex of inward joy and thankfulness to God, the Giver of all good. O! 'tis the merry time wherein honest neighbours make good cheer, and God is glorified in his blessings upon the earth.

PETER PARLEY   *Peter Parley's Annual*, 1854

Giving a penny to the crossing sweeper

A Scene of Distress

An open gate hard by, leading to a sort of shed, seemed to invite him to enter; and his ear now, for the first time, caught the sound of the anvil, to him well-known. He had not before noticed it, because its clink, clink, had mingled with the song of the bird, the bleating of sheep, the ripple of the stream, and the many pleasant sounds which gave life and harmony to the scene. He entered the shed, but it entirely changed the bent of his thoughts and feelings. It was humble, and spoke of toil; but it was not that which pained him so.

He had been a blacksmith himself in his earlier days, and had worked very hard to earn a living, but many who work for their bread as he had done, with a contented spirit, are more happy than those who have nothing to do. What was it, then, that grieved him so much in this little shed? It was the ignorance and disease he saw there.

A middle-aged man, and a boy about nine years old, were at work there making nails; they were what is called 'nailors' . . . Well, the man we were telling you of was poor, and had a large family to provide for, so he had been obliged to take his little boy, almost from his mother's arms, and set him to work, to help to earn money to buy their food. He was then too little to reach his father's block, so a large stone was placed for him to stand on. And that cold damp stone, and the want of proper air and exercise, had stopped the poor child's growth, and made him sickly, so that years after he needed the stone to raise him, as much as when he was first placed on it. Then he was very ignorant, for his parents could neither spare the time nor the money to send him to school; so he was to be pitied, not blamed for it.

Dear little readers, there are very many such cases. Thousands of children are obliged to work for ten hours a day in a factory or workshop. Now, suppose that, for one week, you were sent to a place where instead of being in a nice house you would be obliged to live crowded together, eight or ten persons perhaps in one room, and that instead of having nice meals of meat and pudding, and all sorts of good things, as most of you have now, you had nothing but dry bread, and not so much as you could eat of that. Then, suppose, that instead of going to school and learning to read and write, and such things, and after school hours are over running about and playing, full of health and strength, you were obliged to work hard all day until you were so tired that you had no spirit for anything, but were glad to

RICH, THOUGH POOR.

lie down anywhere and go to sleep, from fatigue, having made
you unable to bestir yourself.

You think that we have drawn a very dreadful picture, and so
we have; but it is a true one, and if you would shrink from one
week spent in that manner, what must it be to always live in
that way? You know what we said about all being brethren –
these poor little factory children and nailors are your brothers
and sisters, and we want you to feel for them, and to help them
in every way you can.

MISS WINNARD *Fanny and Arthur*

Vulgar Little Lady

'But, mamma, now,' said Charlotte, 'pray, don't you believe
That I'm better than Jenny, my nurse?
Only see my red shoes, and the lace on my sleeve;
Her clothes are a thousand times worse.

'I ride in my coach and having nothing to do,
And the country folks stare at me so;
And nobody dares to control me but you,
Because I'm a lady, you know.

'Then, servants are vulgar, and I am genteel;
So, really, 'tis out of the way,
To think that I should not be better a deal
Than maids, and such people as they.'

'Gentility, Charlotte,' her mother replied,
'Belongs to no station or place;
And nothing's so vulgar as folly and pride,
Though dress'd in red slippers and lace.'

'Not all the fine things that fine ladies possess
Should teach them the poor to despise;
For 'tis in good manners, and not in good dress,
That the truest gentility lies.'

ANON   *Original Poems*, 1868 Edition

Workhouse Children

I think it may be interesting to your readers, to know how
much pleasure may be given, by following out Mrs Sewell's
admirable advice, given in the 'Children's Friend' for December, 1862.
She recommends children to send their *old toys*, etc., to the
workhouse near them.
My children have, each Christmas-eve since then, sent off a
large hamper of toys, pictures, little books, a few nuts, oranges,
and sweetmeats, to our Union Workhouses, for the poor little
children who have so few joys; and each year we get such a
thankful letter from the wife of the Chaplain of the Union,

telling us that our hamper has given great delight to *all* the inmates, the old people rejoicing for the children's sakes.

It has occurred to me that this year we might also send a few comforts, such as a little tea, sugar, or knitted stockings, for the *aged*. The pleasure that the packing and collecting of the goods occasions is very great to my children, and the expense is so very trifling, that I think there can be no nursery unable to afford it.

I have no doubt numbers of your readers have done as we have done; but with the hope that some may again be stirred up, by hearing of the success in our Union, I venture to trouble you with these few lines.

With the heartfelt hope, that you and Mrs Sewell may live long to be a continued blessing to children,

I remain, yours truly,
'S'

ANON   *The Children's Friend*, December 1865

The Village Green

On the cheerful village green,
Skirted round with houses small,
All the boys and girls are seen,
Playing there with hoop and ball.

Now they frolic hand in hand,
Making many a merry chain;
Then they form a warlike band,
Marching o'er the level plain.

Now ascends the worsted ball,
High it rises in the air,
Or against the cottage wall,
Up and down it bounces there.

Then the hoop, with even pace,
Runs before the merry throngs;
Joy is seen in every face,
Joy is heard in cheerful songs.

THE WIDOW AND HER SON.

Rich array, and mansions proud,
Gilded toys, and costly fare,
Would not make the little crowd
Half so happy as they are.

Then, contented with my state,
Where true pleasure may be seen,
Let me envy not the great,
On a cheerful village green.

ANON *Original Poems*, 1868 Edition

Ann and her Mamma

Little Ann and her Mother were walking one day
Through London's wide city so fair,
And business obliged them to go by the way
That led them through Cavendish Square.

And as they pass'd by the great house of a Lord,
A beautiful chariot there came,
To take some most elegant ladies abroad,
Who straightway got into the same.

The ladies in feathers and jewels were seen,
The chariot was painted all o'er,
The footmen behind were in silver and green,
The horses were prancing before.

Little Ann by her Mother walk'd silent and sad,
A tear trickled down from her eye,
Till her Mother said, 'Ann, I should be very glad
To know what it is makes you cry.'

'Mamma,' said the child, 'see that carriage so fair,
All covered with varnish and gold,
Those ladies are riding so charmingly there,
While we have to walk in the cold.'

'You say GOD is kind to the folks that are good,
But surely it cannot be true;
Or else I am certain, almost, that He would
Give such a fine carriage to you.'

'Look there, little girl,' said her Mother, 'and see
What stands at that very coach door;
A poor ragged beggar, and listen how she
A halfpenny tries to implore.

'All pale is her face, and deep sunk is her eye,
And her hands look like skeleton's bones;
She has got a few rags, just about her to tie,
And her naked feet bleed on the stones.'

A morning gallop

' "Dear ladies," she cries, and the tears trickle down,
"Relieve a poor beggar, I pray;
I've wander'd all hungry about this wide town,
And not ate a morsel to-day.

' "My Father and Mother are long ago dead,
My brother sails over the sea,
And I've scarcely a rag, or a morsel of bread,
As plainly, I'm sure, you may see.

' "A fever I caught, which was terribly bad,
But no nurse or physic had I;
An old dirty shed was the house that I had,
And only on straw could I lie.

' "And now that I'm better, yet feeble and faint,
And famish'd, and naked, and cold,
I wander about with my grievous complaint,
And seldom get aught but a scold.

' "Some will not attend to my pitiful call,
Some think me a vagabond cheat;
And scarcely a creature relieves me, of all
The thousands that traverse the street.

' "Then ladies, dear ladies, your pity bestow. " '
Just then a tall footman came round,
And asking the ladies which way they would go,
The chariot turn'd off with a bound.

'Ah! see, little girl,' then her Mother replied,
'How foolish those murmurs have been;
You have but to look on the contrary side,
To learn both your folly and sin.

'This poor little beggar is hungry and cold,
No mother awaits her return;
And while such an object as this you behold,
Your heart should with gratitude burn.

'Your house and its comforts, your food and your friends
'Tis favour in GOD to confer;
Have you any claim to the bounty He sends,
Who makes you to differ from her?

'A coach, and a footman, and gaudy attire,
Give little true joy to the breast;
To be good is the thing you should chiefly desire,
And then leave to GOD all the rest.'

ANON   *Poll Parrot Picture Book*

The Cottage Girl

Mrs Sherwin called, in her coach, and took Milly with her to
her own house. She was here presented to Grace Sherwin, a
girl somewhat older than herself, and was told that her particular duty was to attend upon her. Grace received her kindly,
and very soon took her into the garden, and showed her over
the grounds about the house. . . .
Returning from this ramble, the girls went to a play-room
fitted up for Miss Grace's own use, for she was an only child,
and everything that wealth could obtain for her amusement
was freely purchased. Here was collected a great quantity of

The Rent paid costly toys, among which were a beautiful doll, a curtained bed and a great variety of articles, making up a complete set of little furniture, and all arranged in proper order. The doll was dressed like a fine lady, and seated in a cushioned chair, lined with pink satin. She was attended by two doll waiting maids, who seemed to watch her ladyship and stand ready to do everything she desired to have done. By her side was a shaggy little dog, with bright eyes and silky hair; and at a short distance was a negro boy, holding a pony, as if expecting that his mistress would go forth and take a ride.

Poverty and Riches

Milly thought she had never seen anything so charming as these toys. They next went to Grace's sleeping-room, and there Grace showed Milly her dresses, which included at least twenty frocks, of costly materials, with a number of other articles.

At first Milly was treated by Grace as an equal, and one whom she desired to please and dazzle with the beautiful things she possessed. But in a few days her manner was changed, and Milly was made to feel that she was not an equal but a dependant, and one who was expected to submit to every whim and caprice of her young mistress. Now Milly, like Grace, was an only child, and had never been accustomed to look upon herself as an inferior: but her family was poor, and she had not been indulged with having all the fine things she might desire, nor had she been accustomed to be surrounded with those who obeyed every wish and flattered every fancy.

At first, therefore, she felt pained to see herself treated as an inferior and a menial; and a kind of discontent crept over her heart to see how rich and cherished was her young mistress, while she was so poor and dependent, and so little cared for. Under the influence of these feelings, the Cottage Girl became home-sick, and stealing away to her own room, she buried her face in her hands and burst into a flood of tears. Oh, how she longed to see her mother; how she yearned to go back again to her simple home; and how much more dear to her heart were its naked beams and sanded floors, with father and mother, than the stately apartments, and turkey carpets, and gorgeous furniture of the great house of Sherwin Hall!

Milly sat for some time in her room, and had opportunity to reflect upon a lesson which it is well for us all to learn; that happiness lies in the heart, and not in the things by which we are surrounded; that the bosom, if contented and at ease, may be blessed in a cottage, while it may be miserable in the midst of every luxury.

PETER PARLEY *Cheerful Cherry*

The Rich Girl and the Poor Boy

JULIA
'We must not play together,
Tom Smith, I'm very sure;
For my papa is very rich
And yours is very poor.'

THOMAS
'But my papa is honest,
A good and useful man,
In what is yours the better,
Pray tell me, if you can?'

JULIA
'He's very rich, I tell you:
Now, Tom, what would you give,
If in a house as grand as ours
Your own papa could live?'

THOMAS
'I would not give a sixpence;
For, though your house be higher,
'Tis just as likely to blow down,
Or be burnt up by fire.

'Amongst your fine rich furniture
You cannot eat in peace;
Lest on your Brussels carpet you
Should get a spot of grease.'

JULIA
'But, Tom, look at your coarse thick coat,
Then at my dress so fine;
What would you give if you could wear
Clothes half so rich as mine?'

THOMAS
'I would not give a farthing,
Whatever you may think,
For finery that may be spoiled
By every drop of ink.

Poverty and Riches

'My clothing is my comfort,
And in comfort is it worn:
I'm not, like you, in constant fear
Lest it get soiled or torn.

'Thanks to my best of mothers,
My dress is whole and clean;
Nor do I wish to change it
For the gayest ever seen.

'And, for my dear good father –
As I have said before –
Yours may, perhaps, be richer,
But you cannot love him more.

'Nor is he more respected:
Such is my father's worth –
His children would not change him
For the richest man on earth.

'You boast your father's fortune –
And rich enough is he;
With his fine houses here in town,
And vessels out at sea.

'But many as rich a merchant,
And prosperous as he,
Have, by misfortune, been reduced
To utter poverty.

'Your vessels may be shipwrecked,
Your houses may burn down;
And you may find yourself at last
The poorest girl in town.

'If you have nought but riches
To pride yourself upon,
You'll be a very wretched Miss,
When all your wealth is gone.

*An Etonian and his
sisters*

'Virtue, be sure, and learning,
Are treasures of more worth,
Than all the gold that ever men
Have hoarded upon earth.

'For when the fire or tempest
Take other wealth away,
Our knowledge and our goodness then
Are treasures that will stay.

'And one thing more I'll tell you –
Deny it, if you can;
'Tis honesty and goodness
That woman makes, or man.'

When this was uttered, Julia
A pretty curtsey made;
And said, 'I thank you, little boy,
For all that you have said.'

And then approached him kindly,
And took him by the hand,
And said, 'I'll value goodness more
Than money, house, or land.'

PETER PARLEY *Peter Parley's Magazine*, 1845

Sad Hearts in Grand Houses

BETTER is little with the fear of the LORD, than great treasure and trouble therewith. Proverbs, chapter XV,V,16.

In the fine house . . . there lives a man whose only son is just dead. Do you see them carrying poor Baby to the grave? In the cottage lives a poor woman who has many happy, strong children. Which is the happier – the poor woman or the rich man? I am sure I know that you will answer – the poor woman! And it is well to remember that riches cannot give happiness; that many a sad heart is to be found in a grand house, and many a merry one in a poor cottage. But neither in a cottage, nor in a grand house, can people be happy unless they love and fear GOD.

LOVE GOD, and every thing He sends will be
A blessing, whether known or hid from thee.

ANON   *Proverbs of Solomon*

HIGH DAYS & HOLIDAYS

The rare holiday pleasures of the working classes were dictated by what the ruling classes thought was good for them. Evangelical patronage became more organised as working hours grew shorter. Youngsters were to be kept usefully out of mischief at the YMCA (1844), the YWCA (1855) and later in the century in the Brigades and the Friendly Societies.

Eventually when workers had more money, energy and independence the commercialisation of leisure took care of their spare time. The self-starters in urban communities were the Trades Unions with their Brass Bands, Choral Societies and Institutes. A century ago leisure activities were as much an indication of social status as they are now. No Church, Union or philanthropic patron started people off on golf, bridge and sailing.

The position of middle-class children in the sphere of leisure was perfectly clear. The place for private personal enjoyment was the home. They might enjoy, with indulgence, the spectacle of poor children skirmishing in the streets. But their job was to be seen in public on community occasions, helping the less fortunate to enjoy themselves – not by mixing, but by providing the means. The pleasure gained was the gratitude expected.

They were being trained for their philanthropic rôle. Part of grown-up work might look like pleasure, but it was really responsibility for other people's leisure. In this field, as in all others, moral duty came first.

New Year's Day

Old Father Time has with his scythe mown down all the flowers, the weeds, and the thorns of the old year, and with them its cares and sorrows; and the new year, like a child just born, comes forth naked but full of hope.

Therefore, All hail, to thee, January! cold and wintry as thou art, if it be but in virtue of thy first day. The day, as the French call it *par excellence, le jour de l'an.* Come about me, all ye little schoolboys that have escaped from the unnatural

The local fair

thraldom of your last wash! come crowding about me, with your untamed hearts, shouting with your unmodulated voices, and your happy spirits dancing an untaught measure in your eyes. Come and help me to speak the praises of a New-year's day – one of the *three* which have of late been yours almost exclusively, and which have bettered you and which have bettered themselves by the change: Christmas day which *was*, and New-Year's day which *is*, and Twelfth day which is to be. Let us compel them all three into our presence, and with a whisk of our imagination convert them into one, as the conjuror does his three glittering balls, and then enjoy them all together on this day, with all their dressings, and coachings, and visitings, and greetings, and gifts, and 'many happy

returns;' and their plum-puddings, and mince-pies, and twelfth-
cakes, and negus; with their forfeits, and fortune-tellings, and
blind-man's buff, and sittings-up to supper; and their panto-
mimes and panoramas, and new penknives, and gifts of
Parley's Annual to make them wiser and better, and to turn
young life into a perpetual holiday. This is our New-year's
music; so pipe up, my little ones, and be ye merry.

WILLIAM MARTIN (Ed.)   *Peter Parley's Annual*, 1866

Fanny's Birthday

In the meanwhile, Fanny's birthday approached, and as it was
within a few days of that of her cousin, Emma Delmont, it was
agreed to celebrate the two festivals together. Double feasting!
double holiday! double presents! never was a gayer anniversary.
Mrs Delmont's own gifts had been reserved to the conclusion
of the jollity, and after the fruit was put on the table, two
huge dolls, almost as big as real babies, were introduced to the
little company. They excited and deserved universal admira-
tion. The first was a young lady of the most delicate construction and most elaborate ornament; a doll of highest fashion,
with sleeves like a bishop, a waist like a wasp, a magnificent
bustle, and petticoats so full and so puffed out round the
bottom, that the question of hoop or no hoop was stoutly
debated between two of the older girls. Her cheeks were very
red, and her neck very white, and her ringlets in the newest
possible taste. In short, she was so completely *à la mode* that
a Parisian milliner might have sent her as a pattern to her
fellow tradeswoman in London, or the London milliner might
have returned the compliment to her sister artist over the
water. Her glories, however, were fated to be eclipsed. The
moment that the second doll made its appearance, the lady of
fashion was looked at no longer.
The second doll was a young gentleman, habited in the striped
and braided costume which is the ordinary transition dress of
boys between leaving off petticoats and assuming the doublet
and hose. It was so exactly like Willy Delmont's own attire,
that the astonished boy looked at himself, to be sure that the

84

A little party at the big house

doll had not stolen the clothes off his back. The apparel, however, was not the charm that fixed the attention of the young people; the attraction was the complexion, which was of as deep and shining a black, as perfect an imitation of a negro, in tint and feature, as female ingenuity could accomplish. The face, neck, arms, and legs were all covered with black silk; and much skill was shown in shaping and sewing on the broad flat nose, large ears, and pouting lips, whilst the great white teeth and bright round eyes relieved the monotony of the colour. The wig was of black worsted, knitted and then unravelled, as natural as if it had actually grown on the head. Perhaps the novelty (for none of the party had seen a black doll before) might increase the effect, but they all declared that they had never seen so accurate an imitation, so perfect an illusion. Even Fanny, who at first sight had almost taken the doll for her old enemy Pompey in little, and had shrunk back accordingly, began at last to catch some of the curiosity (for curiosity is a catching passion that characterised her companions). She drew near – she gazed – at last she even touched the doll, and listened with some interest to Mrs Delmont's detail of the trouble she found in constructing the young lady and gentleman.

'What are they made of, aunt?'

'Rags, my dear!' was the reply: 'nothing but rags,' continued Mrs Delmont, unripping a little of the black gentleman's foot and the white lady's arm, and showing the linen of which they were composed; – 'both alike, Fanny,' pursued her good aunt,

'both the same colour underneath the skin, and both the work of the same hand – like Pompey and you,' added she more solemnly; 'and now choose which doll you will.'
And Fanny, blushing and hesitating, chose the black one; and the next day her aunt had the pleasure to see her show it to Pompey over the wall, to his infinite delight; and, in a very few days, Mrs Delmont had the still greater pleasure to find that Fanny Elvington had not only overcome and acknowledged her prejudice, but had given Pompey a new half-crown, and had accepted groundsel for her Canary-bird from the poor negro boy.

MARY RUSSELL MITFORD   *Children of the Village*

Through the stubble to and fro,
Mark the little gleaners go,
Radiant, rosy as the morn,
Seeking for the scattered corn;
Gladsome most when they espy
Where the ears the thickest lie.
See the merry gleaners go,
Through the stubble to and fro.

Prince of Wales' Day

March the First is the Prince of Wales' day. He is the Prince of Welshmen, just as much as St David is their saint; and some day or òther we shall find him having a seat in Wales, just as our good Queen has a seat in Scotland, and then we may expect to see the hills and the valleys, the mountains and the streams, choked with loyal Welsh men and Welsh women going to see the Prince from every village in the Leek Country.

The Welsh boys in London are true ancient Britons. How doggedly do they fag, and how doggedly do they fight! It takes no time to get a Taffy up, but it takes a long time to get him down. You should go to the Welsh Charity School at Ashford, and you will soon see the stuff that Welsh boys are made of. The Prince of Wales is their Patron, and they are proud of it. These juvenile ancient Britons, according to annual custom, go in procession to the Royal residence on St David's day with a copy of *Peter Parley's Annual* under their arms (of course), and receive the Royal bounty. The Society are in carriages, and each wears in his hat an artificial leek which does not smell. They are preceded by marshals on horseback, wearing very much larger leeks in their hats, and are ornamented with silken scarfs. In this array they go to and from the presence of the good Prince, who is as affable as he is generous, and has all the virtues of an ancient Briton. And then the boys have a dinner and leek soup, and a holiday and what not, and go back to school with merry hearts and cheerful countenances.

The First of March is usually rather boisterous, and then it is that the Welsh girls, instead of being feasted by a Prince, are to be seen collecting the sea-wrack on the Welsh coast among the storms and billows; now and then, perhaps, rescuing some shipwrecked mariner from a watery grave. It is then that the leek shines brightest and smells the sweetest; for charity and deeds of mercy are ever fragrant, and rise before the throne of the Invisible like incense.

WILLIAM MARTIN (Ed.) *Peter Parley's Annual,* 1866

The Whiskey is Buoyant

And how is St Patrick's day honoured in London? Well, there are Irish lords and ladies and gentlemen who never forget their country, and as many of the poor who never forget their saint. It is the anniversary of the Benevolent Society of St Patrick, which is duly observed by a feast at one of our large London taverns, and there assemble the Boys belonging to the School, embryo workmen, all clothed down to the ten toes, well-fed and educated also, and as the company arrive, the crowd surround them on every side, and 'largesses' are freely distributed among the halt, the lame and the blind, who are fairly overcome by the 'swate faces' of the ladies and their fair hands 'doing the mercies.'

The day after St Patrick's day is Shelah's day. As to who Shelah was, nobody knows. Some say she was St Patrick's wife; others that she was St Patrick's mother; while all agree that her 'immortal memory' is to be celebrated by the 'immortal hippocrene' whiskey. Then it is, when the whiskey is buoyant, that the 'true' glory of old Ireland becomes manifest. The Shelahs are apt to get a little excited, and then there is a hubbub. Then the men get excited too, and then there is a flourish of cudgels called 'Shelah-lellys;' and then there is a row, a bit of a fight, cracked crowns, and broken noses; in the midst of which the priest appears, and stills the tempest in an instant. The combatants fall on their knees at his bidding, and there is an end of the tumult.

WILLIAM MARTIN (Ed.) *Peter Parley's Annual*, 1866

Easter Monday

Easter Monday is a grand day with all holiday people, and nothing delights me more than to go out on that day, just to look at the thousands of happy faces. In London the streets are thronged with persons of all classes, 'going a pleasuring;' some to the museums, some to the picture galleries, but the greatest numbers, by far, to Greenwich and Hampton Court – almost too cold for picnics, but go they will; and thousands of poor delicate females, stored up in milliners' shops, or in close rooms, singing the death song of the shirt, catch colds that last through the whole summer, the ensuing winter, and kill them in the spring. But then Greenwich Hill has such attractions; and the roll down it is so bewitching, that few can forego the pleasure of it; and away they go in throngs, and shoals. Steam-boats are crammed, cars crammed likewise – and the park is soon crammed also; and the poor unfortunate donkeys on Blackheath are the only animals not benefited by the holiday – but to them it is indeed a 'black Monday.' Good little children, if any of you who read this should go to Greenwich, do not, as you love Peter Parley, encourage, by your pence, the cruel beatings to which these poor animals are subject by their heartless drivers. Can it be pleasure for you to ride the poor beast, while your ears are assailed and your back is shook by the eternal thumpings of heavy cudgels on the nether parts of your bruised steed. Enjoy yourselves, my dear children, but do not let your pleasure be founded upon the pain of others.

PETER PARLEY *Peter Parley's Magazine*, 1845

)ver the hills and far away

MIDSUMMER HOLIDAY

By Ruth Buck

W. & R. CHAMBERS,
LONDON AND EDINBURGH.

May Day Morning

They had saved up money to buy ribbons and strips of coloured cambric to dress up the garland and the children with; for, when their papa gave them leave to have it, he said, as they wished it to be their own treat, it should be given with their own time and money; but, as he intended to give something too, his treat should be a nice tea of cake and buns in the servants' hall, when they came home from their garlanding in the evening.

The almshouse children had been told, that they might have something pleasant to think about too; and oh, what anxiety there was for fear there should be wet weather when it came to the last few days of April! But the sun shone out, and the flowers blossomed, and every afternoon we went for long walks into the country, and brought back such baskets full of them, and kept them in water in cool places against the great day; and a young lady who was staying at the deanery, and heard what was to happen, wrote a little song for the children to join in when they danced round the garland. . . .

On the last day of April I went alone through the little arch, to ask that the children might be spared to come and help make the garland that evening, and to have a whole holiday for the treat the next day; and Alice had promised to go from one house to another and do all the poor people wanted, so that they might not be uncomfortable without their little helpers.

All gave leave, and seemed pleased the children should enjoy themselves, for there was a change since first I went there; and little Rattle sat on her door-step nursing an old doll of Miss Milly's, and Goodie Grunt looked on without scolding at all, for she was much kinder to Dorcas, and began to be called only Goodie, and the ugly word 'Grunt' was dropped altogether.

When it was finished, ours was a garland! I have never seen one like it, before or since, so large and beautiful, and rich with dewy flowers. Alice had been so clever in choosing the prettiest colours to go next each other; and there was a crown of ribbons at the top, and a wax-doll Miss Ada dressed, like a little queen, set inside. And when the gardener came and tied it to the top of a long pole, and uplifted it in the midst of us, there was quite a shout of joy from all the children.

I do not think the birds even opened their eyes on May-day
Left: Title Page morning earlier than my young ladies did; they were up and

dressed before the clatter of little boots and shoes on the stones of the yard told that the almshouse children had gone round the back way to fetch their garland, which had been kept fresh on the bricks of the scullery all night; and by the time Miss Ada was down stairs in the hall, Robin brought it carefully and proudly round to the front of the house, followed by the other children.

Then Alice fetched down the basket of ribbons and strips of cambric; and the young ladies tied sashes of pink round the girls' waists, and pinned bows on their little old-fashioned white caps and aprons, and a blue cambric scarf round Robin's shoulder, and a rosette on his cloth cap. And then he stood in the middle with the garland, and the girls joined hands and danced round in a quiet, measured way, singing their song, and dancing and bowing and curtseying so steadily, and looking somehow, even then, different to all other children. Poor little hearts! such a treat as this was all new to them!

Mr Lee and all the servants came to look at them. Then we threw a shower of pence to begin their day with, and Dorcas made a bob curtsey at us after every single penny she picked up and put into the money-box she carried. . . .

And then they went to all the other houses in Cloister Lane, and then out of the big arch into the streets; and we lost sight of them altogether till late in the afternoon, when they came back hot and happy, and hungry enough, to keep us all busy, handing buns and cake, and bread-and-butter, as they sat at tea round the large oak table in the servants' hall.

When tea was over, I opened the box, and divided the money between them. And only think of there being twenty-eight shillings in it! – four shillings for each child! – enough to give them and their grannies many a little pleasure through the coming year.

ANON *The Nursery Times*

Fred's Letter to his Father

Dear Papa,   *Manchester*
How glad I am that you allowed me to accept uncle Alfred's
invitation! I have only been four days from home, and I am
sure my sheet of paper will not be half large enough to tell
you all I have seen. Our journey from Derby, where we slept,
to this place, was so beautiful, that I wished for you and
mamma, and George, a hundred times to enjoy it with me.
Mr Lincoln told me he generally travelled that road to Manchester on account of its great beauty. I never saw real rocks
before, although I have often read about them. One called
the High Tor, at Matlock, is a noble rock, three or four hundred
feet high, and there is a river running at the foot of it. The
rock seems just as if it had been broken from top to bottom.
In some places you see long slanting lines, as if one part of the
rock had sunk down. But I cannot write anything more of
our journey, because I wish to tell you about the steam-
carriages and the railroad.
Yesterday uncle Alfred took me to the railroad, and he showed
me all the carriages and the steam-engine; and we saw a
Train (as they call six or seven carriages fastened together)
set off. They started very slowly, and presently went along
faster than our coach did when the horses galloped. We saw a
train come in, and they stopped them so gently, that I was
quite astonished; and there was not one passenger that looked
frightened; they all seemed pleased that they had travelled
so fast; then the steam-engine was unfastened from the train,
and the engine man moved it about one hundred yards, till
it came just under a pipe that filled it with water. As soon as
the engine came back, and was hooked to the train again,
my uncle and I got into one of the open carriages; he fixed
upon an open one in order that we might see everything as
well as possible. It was not long before the steam-engine began
to pull very gently all the six carriages with one hundred and
twenty people in them; and then we went faster, faster, faster,
oh, so fast! I wish, dear papa, you had been with us – the
horses galloping with the coach seem like nothing to it. What
a wonderful invention the steam-engine is, and what a clever
thought, to make an iron road for the wheels to run on; but
how much time and labour it must all have cost! At one place
they have made the road over a great black swampy place
five miles long, by putting down many thousand loads of
gravel. At another place they have built a great high bridge,

called the Sankey Viaduct, over the Sankey River; and canal barges, with high masts and sails, go under it. At another place they have cut through a hill called Olive Mount; this hill is all stone, but not a hard grey stone like the High Tor at Matlock, but reddish, and looks something like that which grind-stones are made of. All the rock that they cleared out they threw into a valley, and there made a great sloping embankment, at the top of which the rail-road runs. We were only one hour and a quarter going thirty-two miles! There is a mail coach at the end of the train of carriages, which carries the letters between Manchester and Liverpool.

The steam engine

Uncle Alfred has been very kind; he has explained to me the steam-engine, and I have written down in my book all I can remember; and I think I can explain it even so that George may understand it. Uncle Alfred is not offended if I do not understand him immediately, and therefore I do not mind asking him questions. I never can understand the explanation of a person who looks as if he thought I was stupid all the time I am speaking.

I wish I could draw like uncle Alfred. When he sketches a machine for me, he makes me understand it quite clearly; so that I do not feel afraid that I shall not understand a thing even if it does seem difficult at first. I could not help laughing when uncle Alfred said a steam-engine was something like a squirt; but it is indeed, papa, as I will show you when I come home, for I have got it down in my book.

Your affectionate Son

'FRED

ANON   *The Parent's Cabinet* 1868 [reprinted]

Ellen's Party

One morning, when we were gathered round the breakfast table, Mrs Grey said, 'Ellen, next Thursday will be your birthday, and as it is always customary for you to have some unusual pleasure on such occasions, your papa and I have determined that you shall this time choose your own treat. You need not decide now, my dear, you had better take a little time to think about it.' 'Oh, thank you, dear mamma,' said Ellen, 'I think I am quite sure what I should like, if papa and you have no objection.' 'Tell us what it is,' said the Vicar, 'and if your request is reasonable I am sure neither your mamma nor I will object?' 'Well, then,' said Ellen, 'I should like to have all the school children to tea upon the lawn, and to give them a book each; you know I can buy them with my own pocket-money, and I am sure it will please them so.' 'Very well, dear,' said her parents, 'we will think about it.' The eyes of Ellen were over-flowing with tears. 'What is the matter, my dear?' said Mrs Grey, 'we have not denied you your request.' 'Oh, no, dear, dear Mamma,' was the child's reply. 'I was thinking of something quite different. I was thinking how very good God is to me in having given me such dear kind parents.'
'Not more than others I deserve,
Yet God has given me more.'
'I am glad you feel grateful, my love,' said her father, 'but you must show your gratitude by actions as well as words, when you have it in your power.' I left the room soon after, having learned another lesson from this infant Christian; I felt how ungrateful I had been for all my mercies.

The day before the fete, Ellen engaged us all to assist in the preparations; swings were to be erected, a tent was to be raised, and garlands of flowers were to be placed here and there, in order to make the scene as gay as possible. The delight of the little queen of the day knew no bounds; but there was no selfishness mixed with her pleasure; she thought more of the gratification which it would afford the children than of her own. 'How delighted they will be, Mr Thompson, when they see the swings,' said she. 'I hope the day will be fine.' The day arrived, and I think we elder folks were as well pleased as Ellen, to see that it was favourable. She and John were busied all the morning in gathering flowers, and making garlands, and Mrs Grey, with the female servants, was engaged in preparing cakes and other niceties for the children. At length the appointed hour arrived, and on looking down the road we

saw the procession coming towards the house, headed by the
master and mistress of the school. Ellen spied them first, and
cried, 'Papa, Mamma, here they come; how happy they all
look, and they have all got bouquets of flowers! Look Mr
Thompson, look John;' and away she ran to meet her little
guests. As they passed her two and two, they curtsied, and each
received some kind word in return. When they were seated
round the table, Ellen discovered that a girl named Mary
Wilson was not come, and, upon asking the mistress where she
was, was informed that the girl had stolen something from one
of the children, and to hide her fault had told a falsehood; as
this was not her first offence, the mistress thought the most
effectual way of punishing her would be to forbid her going to
celebrate Miss Ellen's birthday. The face of Ellen wore a look
of deep sorrow, on her hearing this account of the girl's mis-
conduct; but the happy faces around soon attracted her attention; and, indeed, the whole was a pleasing, and unto me a
novel sight. Mr and Mrs Grey were seated at the head of the
table, Ellen and myself on either side, the children were
arranged in order, all around was happiness and smiles, and
plates of cake and fruit were very speedily demolished. The
children came forward, one by one, to receive their present.
I saw an expression of pain pass over the features of Ellen,
when she perceived that there was one book left, but she said
nothing. The children all dispersed to their amusements, and

Buy my Shells.

A day by the seaside

we felt great pleasure in witnessing their happiness. Just before the children left, Ellen came into the parlour with a little note, and the book which had been left in her hand. She said, 'Mamma, I wish to send this book to Mary Wilson.' 'But why send it to her, my dear?' said her mamma; 'she has acted very wrong, and I think it will appear like rewarding vice.' 'I thought of sending this note with it, mamma; then I think she cannot imagine that I mean it as a reward.' She gave the note to her mother, who read it aloud.

'MARY WILSON, I am very sorry that you have acted in such a manner as to oblige the good mistress of the school to forbid your coming to celebrate my birthday; you have been guilty of two great sins, but I hope this is the last time you will suffer yourself to be led into temptation. I hope God will forgive you; I will pray for you, and you must pray for yourself. I send you this little book that you may remember me, and I hope the next birthday I keep you will be able to come. ELLEN GREY.'

'I think you may venture to send that, Ellen,' said Mrs Grey; 'it may have a good effect, if the girl has a heart capable of appreciating your kindness; though I fear from what the mistress says, she is inclined to be very wicked. We should not always discard those who have acted wrong, but try to lead them back to virtue; and few hearts are so hard as entirely to resist kindness. Send it then, my dear, and may God bless your feeble effort, and accept your good intention.'

ANN THORP *Aunt Kate's Story*, 1846

The Harvest Home

... Neither was less business going on in the best kitchen than without; first, there was Mrs Elmore herself, armed with her large bunch of keys, of which she seemed always to be selecting one for especial use; and then there was some one always chopping or beating eggs; and another always moving some kettle or saucepan on the hearth; and there was a constant noise of the smoke-jack in the wide chimney, under the pressure of a tremendous piece of beef, which caused every black wheel in the higher regions to utter sounds not unlike the skirlings of an ill-conditioned pipe. The very dogs seemed to be on the alert, and from always being in the way, received many a kick, which sent them yelping into other parts of the busy scene. And as the hours advanced, and the report arrived from the fields respecting the progress of the work in that quarter, the fervour of preparation became hotter, and the old and the young ran faster and got more and more into each other's way, till at length Mrs Elmore, coming to a stand in the very middle of the kitchen, gave one scientific glance around her, and exclaimed, 'They may come now as soon as they will; if nothing has been forgotten, we are all ready.' 'And so we be,' cried old Betty, 'the best table and all set off with flowers as fine as a May-pole, thanks to Miss Harriet and them without, just as fine; and if madam has not provided a supper fit for a king, why then my old age has taken away my understanding of such things.'

Whilst the farmer and his men were unloading the last waggon, the supper was being set upon the tables, and the poor women and children ranged in their places in the yard. The great table within the kitchen was kept for the elders of this humble

The reaper and his friends

THE HARVEST HOME.

assembly, many of whom used to reckon up with great delight
the many times in which they had been admitted to sit down
at the same board with their masters and their families, for
some remembered the father, and even the grand-father of
Mr Elmore.

It was most pleasant to the master and mistress to observe
how much the good fare was enjoyed, and still more, to see
how modestly and thankfully every favour was received by the
poor guests. When every one was satisfied, the company went
out into the yard, where Mr Elmore, before he left them to the
enjoyment of some little amusement which had been provided
for them with their wives and children, addressed them, and
called on them to thank God, who, after having shown his
power to withhold the means of plenty, had then in his infinite
mercy opened his hand to supply their necessities in rich
abundance.

ANON *Green's Nursery Annual,* 1848

Mop Fair

'The Mop' was a strange institution to me, and I inquired what it meant.

Mr Elton laughed. 'Oh,' said he, 'it is a statute fair, but held after Michaelmas. It is called a 'Stattis' before Michaelmas, and a 'Mop' afterwards. We hire our servants there for the year. It is the servants' carnival.'

'A strange custom,' said my uncle, 'to remain intact in the nineteenth century.'

'Why, yes,' replied Mr Elton; 'but the servants must have a holiday, and until a fresh scheme is adopted, they will remain true to the annual statutes. It is for the want of the day's amusement that the various " Servants' Registration Societies" have failed. They cannot go to the sea-side, to Scotland, or even take an excursion ticket; so they take and enjoy the only real holiday they have.'

'By all means let us see "ye manners and customs of ye Englishe" in the nineteenth century,' said my uncle, as the relics of the lunch were passed over to old Jack and the attendants.

'Shall you go, Jack,' I asked.

'I never miss, Master Harry,' said Jack; 'I go and see all the shows, and the Mollies and Johnnies enjoying themselves.'

A covey of partridges interrupted our conversation, and we enjoyed the sport until the late dinner was ready.

The morning of the statute fair was, fortunately, fine – one of those delightful days which remind us of the delights of the Indian summer, bright, yet balmy and cool – as we passed along the green, shady lanes, by honeysuckled cottages, past groups of servants in their best clothes, who touched their hats, on to the broad turnpike, which exhibited an unwonted liveliness from the number of vehicles which were on it, all bound to the tall spire of the little market town.

The dull and sleepy town of Stockington was alive that day. The market-place usually so desolate, was filled with stalls, shows, and people. On the other side of the market-house, where truly the 'Stretching canvas formed the gaudy street,' there were more exhibitions, more shows, more people, more stalls. The shop windows glittered with burnished glass and resplendent finery, and the brightest of bright colours. The wonderful ribands, gay prints, shiny billy-cock hats, gorgeous waistcoats, and exceedingly yellow neckerchiefs, were amongst the least of the treasures exhibited to catch the bucolic mind. The public-houses were already filled with customers, though the hiring had hardly commenced. By the side of the market-house the servants stood in rows like the rank and file of an army. Here were shepherds with pastoral crooks in their hands, and a little bit of wool tucked beneath the bands of their rough beaver hats. The shepherds generally wore the neatly-plaited and embroidered smock frocks, while the cowherds and ploughmen shone in all the glory of velveteens, and had a bit of cowhair or whipcord to distinguish their vocation. A bit of finely-twisted silk whipcord also distinguished the waggoners. On the contrary, the servant girls had no distinguishing mark to indicate their calling; though, by some inscrutable means, the masters and mistresses seemed to know who had been hired, and who were still wanting places. Dairymaids and general servants were most in demand. The noise and confusion of this Babel was very great. Sounds the most incongruous struck the ear in every variety of noisy discord.

TOM BURGESS *Every Boy's Annual*, 1871

A day at the races

The blind pointer

Thanksgiving Day

This is a New England festival, usually taking place in November, and was originally designed to commemorate the safe arrival of the Pilgrim Fathers after their stormy wintery passage from England to this country. It is now almost a national anniversary, being observed in a large portion of the states.

It is, in fact, a sort of American Christmas, and as it comes in the season of plenty, it is also the season of charity and good will to men: may we not add, of true thanksgiving to GOD? The rich seldom forget the poor on this day, and, happily in our country, few persons are without their roast turkeys and their pumpkin pies.

The following spirited song gives an idea of the manner in which the day is celebrated:

Come, uncles and cousins –.come, nieces and aunts;
Come, nephews and brothers – no won'ts and no can'ts:
Put business, and shopping, and school-books away;
The year has rolled round – it is Thanksgiving Day!

Come home from the college, ye ringlet-haired youth;
Come home from your factories, ANN, KATY, and RUTH,
From the anvil, the counter, the farm, come away –
Home, home with you, home – it is Thanksgiving Day.

Thanksgiving Day

The table is spread, and the dinner is dressed –
The cooks and the mothers have all done their best:
No Caliph of Bagdad e'er saw such display,
Or dreamed of a treat like Thanksgiving Day.

Pies, puddings, and custards, pigs, oysters, and nuts –
Come forward and take without ifs or buts;
Bring none of your slim, little appetites here –
Thanksgiving Day comes only once in a year!

Now children revisit the darling old place –
Now brothers and sisters long parted, embrace;
The family ring is united once more,
And the same voices shout at the old cottage door!
The grandfather smiles on the innocent mirth,
And blesses the power that has guarded his hearth;
He remembers no trouble, he feels no decay,
But thinks his whole life has been Thanksgiving Day!

Then praise for the past and the present we sing,
And trustful await what the future may bring;
Let doubt and repining be banished away,
And the whole of our lives be a Thanksgiving Day!

S. G. GOODRICH   *Juvenile Forget-Me-Not*, 1858

A game of forfeits

Fifth of November

Ay! those were something like Guy Fawkes days, for we
knew every farmer we visited; and in every house found a
warm welcome; and the old grandmother would rise from her
wicker-chair, beside the ingle, and take her horn-tipped staff
in her hand, and give her spectacles an extra rub as she went
out to take a survey; while she told us what Guys she had
seen fifty years ago, and what a holiday the Fifth of November
was then, when every body, who had any religion at all, went
to church in the morning, and helped to burn Guy Fawkes at
night; and how the old parish-clerk composed a new psalm for
that day, as he thought the old one was not good enough;
and that when he got up to give it out, none of them could
sing for laughing, as he had made the last line much too short,
and to eke it out was compelled to say,
'Twas on this day, this very day,
When villains did conspire,
To blow up the House of Parliament,
With gun-de-pow-de-hire.'

THOMAS MILLER   *The Boy's Own Country Book*

Our Christmas at Home

We had been very merry all day, and, as soon as the lights
were brought in at tea-time, we came trooping into the parlour
from all parts of the house – some from the dairy, where
Mary had been making butter; others from the nursery,
where they had been playing at soldiers; and the rest from
the apple-store over the stable and the school-room, then
used only as a play-room, it being holiday time.
We were all assembled in the parlour, and, after tea, my
mother told us that we might have a game at romps. We
needed no second bidding, and so to play we went in good
earnest. We played at Hunt the Slipper and Forfeits, and I
don't know how many other games, till we were called into
the kitchen for a dance. A good old country dance it was, in
which the family, servants, and all joined, noisily enough –
all but my mother, who sat under a sort of arbour of holly and
other green leaves – for there were always plenty of green leaves

THE CHRISTMAS VISIT.

and red berries to be got in the garden and orchard, however severe the winter might be – and encouraged us with kind words and beaming smiles. After we were tired of dancing – which was not soon, I assure you – a great china bowl of raisins was brought in by John the butler, who acted occasionally as gardener and coachman as well, and was, in fact, a sort of Jack-of-all-trades. What fun there was, to be sure as we ran dancing and singing round the lighted bowl, snatching the plums from the blue flames of the burning spirit, till they were all gone and the blue flames burned themselves out. Well, Snap-dragon over, we had kisses under the Mistletoe; and I recollect quite well how we all laughed when Papa took Betty the cook under the white-berried bough and gave her a great loud kiss.

But our fun had not yet ended. At a signal from my mother we followed her into the dining-room on the other side of the passage. Here a sight awaited us that surprised us one and all. The room was brilliantly lighted up with wax candles on sconces from the walls; and on the table in the centre there was placed a great Christmas Tree, hung all over with little lamps and bon-bons, and toys and sweetmeats and bags of cakes. It was the first tree of the kind that I and my companions had ever seen. It was quite a new-fashion the Christmas Tree; and my brother Tom, who had just come home from Germany, had superintended its getting up and decoration. With what shouts of joy we hailed the pretty Christmas Tree, and with what glee and laughter we began to search among its twinkling lights and bright green leaves for the toys and sweetmeats that were hanging there, each one with a name written on its envelope, I can hardly tell you. But we were very merry, I know, and very grateful to our dear mother for her care in providing this delightful surprise as a finish to our merry evening's sports.

ANON *The Christmas Tree*, 1857

More Blessed

In Germany, the children all make it a rule to prepare Christmas presents for their parents, and brothers, and sisters. Even the youngest contrive to offer something. For weeks before the important day arrives, they are as busy as little bees, contriving and making such things as they suppose will be most agreeable.

The great object is to keep each one ignorant of the present he or she is to receive, in order to surprise them when the offering is presented. A great deal of whispering and innocent management is resorted to, to effect this purpose; and their little

'The cause of her fright was a great lobster which had crept
out of the sea and was coming towards her.'
From *The Town and Country Toy Book*

minds are brimful of the happy business.
This is a most interesting and affectionate custom. I wish all
little girls would excercise their ingenuity in making boxes,
baskets, needlebooks, etc., for the same purpose. Their hearts
will be warmed with good feelings, while their fingers are
acquiring skill; and they will find, as the Bible tells them, that
'it is more blessed to give than to receive.'

MRS CHILD   The Girl's Own Book, 1848

Christmas

We shall have sport when Christmas comes,
When 'snap-dragon' burns our fingers and thumbs:
We'll hang mistletoe over our dear little cousins,
And pull them beneath it and kiss them by dozens:
We shall have games at 'Blind Man's Buff,'
And noise and laughter and romping enough.

We'll crown the plum-pudding with bunches of bay,
And roast all the chestnuts that come in our way;
And when Twelfth Night falls, we'll have such a cake
That as we stand round it the table shall quake.
We'll draw 'King and Queen,' and be happy together,
And dance old 'Sir Roger' with hearts like a feather.
Home for the Holidays, here we go!
But this Fast train is really exceedingly slow!

ANON   Home for the Holidays

SCHOOL &
LEARNING

"HE MADE THE GREAT WHALE AND THE ELEPHANT."

Even today, 'educated' people talk of board school, council school, elementary school – quaint, anachronistic terms which betray a social attitude. Is it merely a sign of ignorance of the educational changes which have taken place, or of positive resistance to them? As well they talk of voluntary, British and Foreign, National, or even Ragged or Sunday Schools – sponsored by the Church, where the Poor could be taught to read the Bible and receive the faith, as well as be kept from mischief and temptation on the streets. Parents contributed a little if they could afford to, and from 1833 schools received Government grants. Before it became clear that an organised system was necessary, educating the poor was a religious and moral duty; an outlet for charity.

Middle-class children were brought up to learn that social inferiors were acceptable if they were diligent and acquiescent, and the schoolchild in the charity school could be tolerated if it were clean, orderly and deferential. This attitude is clearly reflected in juvenile fiction of the period. All conform to the standards demanded; the teacher is a symbol of moral worth rather than of intellectual power. This contrasts with the later fashions when non-conformity was all and the teacher was often an object of ridicule.

As the industrial and mercantile middle classes aspired to the gentlemanly education of the Aristocracy, they sent their sons to the great public schools. The stories generated by these strange institutions, which were developing a new character under reformers like Arnold of Rugby, were to be a different matter. With the introduction of organised games (about 1860), the cult of manliness established itself with its attendant stiff upper lip, house loyalties, adulation of the Blue, identification of 'character' with athletic prowess.

Tutors and governesses, living within the household, tended to be the holders of passports to upper-class society without themselves being accepted as members of it.

Generally speaking, a good memory was considered to be the first prerequisite of success. Poetry was for learning by heart. Facts were crammed into young heads like furniture into drawing rooms. Ability, measured by success in competition, was the result of effort, not a gift from God. Failure was the result of lack of diligence: on the other hand, it was an incentive to perseverance. So if you performed badly, you were caught both ways.

At the Great Exhibition

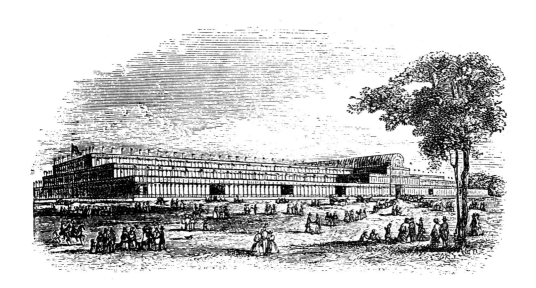

The Crystal Palace from the south west

P: If you come forward a little nearer to the transept, you will see something particularly suited to your taste, Rose.

ROSE: I see what you mean, papa. Here Henry, is a case full of *wax dolls*. Oh papa, I should like to stop here for an hour, I never saw such a number of dolls together before – they are just like a public meeting.

H: And look at that dear little black doll, Rose. The word 'AFRICA,' is written under it.

P: Yes. You may observe that there is one doll from each large division of the globe – one from Europe; another from Africa; and another from America; each doll well represents the character of the race it belongs to. Here is also a small case of rag dolls.

ROSE: They are very beautiful too, papa, they look like wax exactly. Oh, papa, we can never examine all the beautiful things in this building!

P: Do not say 'never,' Rose. You would certainly have to visit the Exhibition a great many times – more than a hundred, perhaps. You may now come with me to examine some cases full of wax flowers.

Here they are! but I cannot let you look at them very long, you would stand round them all the day, and say 'beautiful,' 'beautiful,' until you could not say it any longer.

ROSE: So they are beautiful, papa; lovely! *delicious*!

P: Do not use such a word as that *Rose* – 'delicious' is not used to express any qualities which please the *eye*.

H: No We say – 'delicious taste.'

P: So if you want to express the feelings you have in looking at the Exhibition, you had better keep to the words 'wonderful!' 'beautiful,' 'most beautiful!' — 'magnificent,' 'splendid,' 'most magnificent,' 'most extraordinary' – 'astonishing' – and so on.

H: Well, I should like to make some *new* words; I think that, the things must be tired of hearing those old words said to them so often.

P: True; perhaps they have been uttered some millions of times, they are dropping from the lips of tens of thousands of people all day long.

ROSE: Well, papa – I must say 'beautiful' again, here is a *beautiful* camelia, I will say ' a *magnificent* one,' because it is so large.

P: The truth is, Rose, it is not a camelia at all. It is a new *water lily* of gigantic size, and is truly one of the 'lions' of the Exhibition. You will, I think, say so when you hear its history. It is called THE VICTORIA-REGIA.

You may examine it. Notice its immense leaves, how broad, smooth, and flat they are! The Victoria-Regia has become celebrated not only because of its size, but because it may almost be said to be the *parent* of the Exhibition.

H: How can that be, papa, will you please to tell us?

P: Yes, I have in my pocket a copy of HOUSEHOLD WORDS, in which there is an account of this lily. Let us go a little further to yonder red seats, in the corner of the gallery, we can then look down into the transept.

ROSE: So we can, Henry; and we have come all the way back again to our friend the glass fountain.

P: Now, while you sit here and rest you shall hear a few words concerning the Victoria-Regia . . .

ANON *Little Henry's Holiday at the Great Exhibition*

The Dangers of Cleverness

'Pray, my dear – as I wish to begin from the beginning – who are *we?*' said Mrs Jethro.

'We! – Why the world – people one meets.'

'Very correct diction, I daresay: but, seriously, my dear – have you been in the habit of considering the opinion of 'people you meet,' at the parties you are unfortunately too familiar with, as the best rule for forming your ideas of right and wrong?'

Julia was silent.

'Or think you, my poor child, that it is a proper feeling for a young female to enter life with – that it is (*to use your own words*) '*delightful to be looked at?* – to be a thing stuck up like your own London Monument, or the great gun in the Park – or a performer at a large theatre – for the gaze of the ignorant or vulgar?'

Julia burst into tears. After a pause, she said 'Dear, dear aunt, I only meant to be admired for talent.'

'Believe me, females ought to seek to enliven the domestic circle, by their acquirements; and while they *admire* talent in others, they ought not to be led away by the vain idea of being poets, painters, and musicians *themselves*, merely for the sake of being *admired* – by people who, after all, in nine cases out of ten, know nothing about the matter. Publicity always brings a *large* portion of unhappiness with it. The humble violet, shaded by its broad green leaves, is more secure from danger than the hollyhock, which woos the summer sun.'

'I thought *clever people*, aunt, were always happy.'

MRS S. C. HALL   The Juvenile Budget, 1846

Is Poetry Useful?

Q: Is poetry useful?

A: Yes, so far as it embodies noble and useful sentiments, which excite to virtuous actions and public spirit. Milton, Young, Dryden, Pope, Cowper, and Wordsworth can never be too often read.

Q: Is the art of drawing a desirable acquirement?

A: Yes, nothing more desirable; it teaches us to observe and examine all objects that we see; and it is an inexhaustible source of amusement to ourselves and gratification to our friends.

Q: Is dancing a fit object of education?

A: Dancing adds grace to the person, freedom to the limbs, and health to the body, by its exercise. It is also favourable to friendly association and a source of personal pleasure.

Q: What is the use of music?

A: It is the modifier of sound into melody and harmony, in accordance with our most refined perceptions; and is the most exquisite pleasure of the mind known to man. It is in its practice and perfection the most agreeable of all pastimes.

Q: Is religion a subject for scholastic instruction?

A: None is more so. Every child ought to be exercised in questions on the Old and New Testament; and ought to be able to estimate the moral duties which are inculcated throughout the Sacred Writings.

Q: What ought an educated boy to be familiar with at 15?

A: He ought to read and write well, to be able to calculate in various rules decimally and to work simple equations in algebra; he should be familiar with English grammar and with some foreign language; be able to draw geometrically, and by hand; know geography, history, and biography; and be well practised in book-keeping.

Q: What ought a well-educated girl to have learnt at 15?

A: She ought to read freely in prose or verse; to write grammatically; to be very expert in arithmetic; to know French and Italian; to be familiar with geography, history, and biography; to be mistress of approved and desirable accomplishments; and, above all, to be ready at all kinds of needle-work.

REV. DAVID BLAIR *The Mother's Question Book*

The Virtues of Fagging

Our recollections of this *abominable* institution are mostly of an amusing kind, such as one's fag making tea without having taken the precaution of putting any tea into the teapot, using his master's best trousers for a kettle-holder, and, finally, toasting bread on the spout of a coffee-pot – instances of

Food for the mind

stupidity which one would expect rather from an ignorant Irish housemaid than from an educated English boy; and though we read of the seniors in the 'glorious olden time' sending out their juniors to commit such noble and worthy deeds of heroism as duck-stealing and poaching of every description, in order that the plenteous repast might be served up at the dead of night round the last embers of the expiring fire, and lighted by the solitary tallow candle, which had been carefully concealed for a week before-hand, yet we *read* only; and but few of us can boast of having been implicated in such notable transactions. Picture to yourself the wretched 'lower boy' slowly roasted before the living coals – picture him sleeping in his master's bed, to warm it previous to its reception of its proper owner, or having to sit in during the play-hours to copy out his master's imposition – and then remember that these are fables of the past, too dastardly to be allowed, and too cruel to be inflicted during the present generation. Yes, little boys, tremble, and weep to your mammas your contemplated horrors of being subjected to the most brutal tyranny; and then, when you have come home for the holidays, recount laughingly to your younger brothers how you had only to make your senior's tea in the morning, only keep up his fire during a certain portion of the day; and not even to black his boots, or to brush his clothes.

Seriously speaking, however, in the great public schools this connection is one of mutual benefit, not to mention the incalculable amount of good that has been done to many a lord by his having been put under the authority of those inferior to him by birth. In return for the offices performed by the junior boys for their superiors – not 'menial' or servile offices, but such as can be done without any degradation – the latter not only extend to the former their protection from bullying, but even assist them in any difficulty that may occur in the course of lessons to be learnt, or verses to be done: and naturally taking a deep interest in those for whose career, at this time of life, they are partially responsible, it not unfrequently happens that in after years the 'master' and 'fag' meet together on the most friendly terms, and love to dwell on the reminiscences of the commencement of their mutual attachment under such peculiar circumstances.

EDMUND ROUTLEDGE (Ed.)   *Every Boy's Annual,* 1863

A Lesson Learnt

It happened that about a fortnight after Herbert became an inmate of the Parsonage, a little excursion was planned to visit the ruins of an ancient abbey, situated in a romantic and secluded part of the hills. Herbert was to mount a rough Shetland pony, while the rest of the party, with provisions, etc. were to be conveyed in a humble equipage, namely a covered waggon. As the expedition was not to start until twelve o'clock, the children were required to attend to a part of their lessons previously; as Mr Graham thought that they would enjoy the coming pleasure much more than if they had been idling about all the morning.

Charles was not much disposed to acquiesce with this decision, as his tasks for that day were in the Latin Grammar and Vocabulary, which he had but just commenced; and I am sorry to say, it was with a bad grace that he took his seat with his Papa in the study.

He soon made up his mind that his lessons were too difficult to be learned; and allowing his thoughts to dwell on his expected excursion, his eyes wandered far from his book, and his Papa's warnings were for once quite unheeded. And so the minutes slipped away; and when the waggon and the pony were at the door, and every one else was quite ready, Charles discovered his error, and how much he had lost, for want of a little attention and perseverance.

'Surely, Papa,' argued he, 'if I learn my lessons when I come home, it will do just as well.' – 'No, my dear; it really grieves me to deprive you of what I am sure would give you pleasure; but I should not feel it right to do otherwise, after your sad waste of time this morning; and if you could not fix your thoughts now, much less in the evening when you are fatigued, and when you would have so many things to fill your mind.'

Nature Study in the park

Poor Charles burst into tears as he heard them drive away from the door; and for some time he was inconsolable. But cook, who was now his sole companion, recommended him to dry his eyes and get his lessons quite perfectly; 'and then you know, Master Charles, you can run in the garden and enjoy yourself as well as your sister and brother.' Charles thought that this was good advice; and in a little time he began to act upon it, feeling much happier as he did so.

One by one the difficulties were all mastered, and he wondered how he could have been so foolish before; fresh tears filled his eyes at this thought, but he checked them speedily, determined to take warning another time. He now hastened to put away his books, and ran out into the garden. 'I shall just have time to go to the brook before my dinner is ready,' said he; 'and if I am fortunate enough to make any discoveries, I shall have something to tell, as well as to hear, when Mamma comes home.'

ANON   *Charlie's Discoveries*

'Fear No NME'

I'll sing a song of A B C
(If you will list awhile,
And pay attention unto me)
That may create a smile.
Not many children, I'll suppose,
But do their letters know;
And therefore I shall sing to them
A song of the *Cross row*.

Both U and I with ee's can C
That man is prone to ill,
And that to B or not to B,
Is the 'great question' still.
Would we preserve our character,
And not our minds abuse,
We must be careful not to R,
And mind our P's and Q's.

A man cannot get on in life,
Unless that he is Y Y's;
And to avoid all snares and strife.
Must make use of his I I's.
In bus'ness would he make his way,
And take care not to lose,
He must look sharp to L S D,
And shun the I O U's.

CLUE *A character
immortalised by Cicero*
ANSWER *Catiline*

118

'Fear No NME'

In all that you are called to do,
Endeavour to X L;
For X L N C is a thing
That rarely fails to tell.
Who puzzles much Z is wrong,
Yet be not over dull,
For it must be a wretched thing
To have an M T skull.

B B C as a B C B,
In village or C T;
In quiet temper ever walk,
And life will E C B.
For those that R still feel P T,
And follow on S T;
Do what is right, walk in the light,
And fear no N M E.

Be careful that you shun X S
When you to make S A,
In meal or drink, or every mess
May hasten you D K.
And dying you will leave behind,
Instead of L E G,
To turn the nose and taint the wind,
A rank X U V E.

Make principle your A and Z,
And pattern F E G;
And then your course of duty will
Be right unto a T.
And when that you shall C C's to B
A living N T T,
In this sad world, in that above,
U L live in X T C.

w.m. *The Birthday Gift*, 1861

The Cost of a Ball

'What are you making, mamma?' 'A ball for you, Arthur.'
'What will it be made of, mamma?' 'It will be made of cork,
indian-rubber, cotton, and worsted.' 'Where does cork come
from, mamma?' 'It comes from Italy and Spain.' 'What is
cork, mamma?' 'It is the bark of the cork tree.' 'And what
is indian-rubber, mamma?' 'It is a kind of gum, which issues
from a tree bearing the same name, and is a native of South
America.' 'And what is cotton, mamma?' 'It is the produce
of the cotton-tree, which grows in the West Indies.' 'And
what is worsted, mamma?' 'Worsted is made from wool, the
fleece of sheep, which live in England, you know, Arthur.'
'But, mamma, sheep are not red, and blue, and yellow, and
purple, like that worsted!' 'No, my love, the wool has been
dyed these various colours.' 'What must I give you for making
that nice ball, mamma?' 'You must give me a kiss, my dear,
and tell me from how many countries the various articles
used in making this ball are obtained.' 'Let me see; I'll count,
mamma:–cork, from Spain, one; indian-rubber, from South
America, two; cotton, from the West Indies, three; and worsted,
which we obtain in England, four; mamma.' 'Yes, Arthur, that
is quite correct; and now your ball is ready.' 'Thank you, dear
mamma: now I will give you a sweet kiss.'

MRS JERRAM *Child's Own Story Book*, 1840

The Rational Toy Shop

When Herbert entered 'the rational toy-shop' he looked all
around, and, with an air of disappointment, exclaimed,
'Why, I see neither whips nor horses! nor phaetons, nor
coaches!' – 'Nor dressed dolls!' said Favoretta, in a reproachful
tone – 'nor baby houses!' – 'Nor soldiers – nor a drum!' continued Herbert, – 'I am sure I never saw such a toy-shop,' said
Favoretta; 'I expected the finest things that ever were seen,
because it was such a new shop, and here are nothing but
vulgar-looking things – great carts and wheelbarrows, and
things fit for orange-women's daughters, I think.'
This sally of wit was not admired as much as it would have been
by Favoretta's flatterers in her mother's drawing-room:– her

brother seized upon the very cart which she had abused, and dragging it about the room, with noisy joy, declared he had found out that it was better than a coach and six that would hold nothing; and he was even satisfied without horses, because he reflected that he could be the best horse himself; and that wooden horses, after all, cannot gallop, and they never mind if you whip them ever so much: 'you must drag them along all the time, though you make believe,' said Herbert, 'that they draw the coach of themselves; if one gives them the least push, they tumble down on their sides, and one must turn back, for ever and ever, to set them up upon their wooden legs again. I don't like make-believe horses; I had rather be both man and horse for myself.' Then, whipping himself, he galloped away, pleased with his centaur character.

Whilst Herbert's cart rolled on, Favoretta viewed it with scornful eyes; but at length, cured by the neglect of the spectators of this fit of disdain, she condescended to be pleased, and spied a few things worthy of her notice. Bilboquets, battledores, and shuttlecocks, she acknowledged were no bad things. 'And pray,' said she, 'what are those pretty little baskets, Madame de Rosier? And those others, which look as if they were but just begun? And what are those strings, that look like mamma's bell cords? – and is that a thing for making laces, such as Grace laces me with? And what are those cabinets with little drawers for?'

Madame de Rosier had taken notice of these little cabinets –
they were for young mineralogists; she was also tempted by a
botanical apparatus; but as her pupils were not immediately
going into the country, where flowers could be procured, she
was forced to content herself with such things as could afford
them employment in town. The making of baskets, of bell-
ropes, and of cords for window-curtains, were occupations in
which, she thought, they might successfully employ themselves.
The materials for these little manufactures were here ready
prepared; and only such difficulties were left as children love
to conquer.

MARIA EDGEWORTH   *The Good French Governess*, 1868

For Capitalists and Students

LECTURES

By the ablest Professors.

ENTERTAINMENTS AND EXHIBITIONS

Constantly varied, and most Instructive and Amusing.
MODELS ON THE LARGEST SCALE.

Engineers, Mechanics, Artists, Builders, Chemists, Musicians,
and all Scientific Professionals and Amateurs, will here find
every novelty likely to interest Inventors, Capitalists, or
Students. The ROYAL POLYTECHNIC is the most fre-
quented and most highly-patronised Institution of the kind
in Europe, being invariably visited by all *savans* [*sic*], and
celebrities arriving in London; and as a place of amusement, it
possesses attractions for the general public which are peculi-
arly its own.

Open Daily from 12 till 5, and from 7 till 10 (Saturday included).
ADMISSION TO THE WHOLE, ONE SHILLING.
Schools and Children under Ten years of Age, Half-price.

WILLIAM MARTIN (Ed.)   *Peter Parley's Annual*, 1866

Sewing for the Heathen

Nellie and Marcella were in the same class in the Sunday-school, and their teacher was Miss Drummond. She was a lovely and devoted Christian, and faithfully cultivated the talents God had given her.

One day, she proposed to her scholars that they should meet every Saturday afternoon in the school-room to sew for poor children in heathen lands. The children were delighted with the plan, and most of the parents consented, as Miss Drummond promised always to meet with them, and to be their president. The next Saturday afternoon was impatiently waited for, and at two o'clock you might have seen twenty little girls, in neat dresses and clean aprons, with their needle-books and thimbles in little bags or baskets upon their arms, going to the school-room. Their friend was already there.

When the children had hung up their bonnets, and seated themselves round the room, she said, 'if you wish any one else to be your president, I should be very glad to have you say so.'

'Oh! no, Miss Drummond! we all want *you*,' said one of the oldest girls.

'Well, all who wish me to be president may stand up,' said she. The children all rose together, and she was satisfied that they really preferred her to any one else.

'Now, my dear children, those of you who are willing to do as I desire you, and to obey me, and to keep the rules of the society, will please to rise.' All rose again.

'Very well,' said Miss Drummond, 'we will now talk a little about our object. In almost all places where we have missionaries in heathen lands, there are schools where poor children – boys and girls – are taught to read, and sew, and cypher; and, above all, are taught about their Lord and Saviour Jesus Christ. We can make clothing for the naked ones, so that they may go to school decently dressed; or we may make quilts, and sheets, and pillow-cases for the missionaries themselves, to use in their families, and for the scholars who live with them; or we can make useful things, that would be likely to be bought here, and in about a year, when we have got a good many things made, we can sell them, and then send the money to be used as the missionaries think best.' . . .

You need not be told that all the children were busy that week, and the dolls were robbed of every superfluous bit of calico, or white cloth, or silk, that was laid by for their use; and it was well, on the next Saturday, that Miss Drummond had thought to provide two large pasteboard boxes, for they were filled with the pieces the children brought.

'Oh, Miss Drummond!' said Lucy Marlow, 'here is half-a-crown. I had it to buy a new bonnet-ribbon with, and the old one will do very well. Please take the money.'

'And I,' said Mary Brown, 'did some plain sewing for Mrs Strachen, and I thought I could give sixpence of what I got for it.'

'And I,' said Anna Harris, 'had some money to buy a new book; but the naked and ignorant need it now.' And thus each one made some little sacrifice, and each had brought an offering.

'My dear children,' said Miss Drummond, 'all this pleases me much; but I want each one of you to ask herself, "Why have I given this? Have I done it because the rest of the children were going to do it? Or because I was ashamed not to do it? Have I done it to be praised for my liberality, and to be called a good little girl? Or have I done it because I loved my Saviour, and wished to do His will?"'

The children were silent, for many of them knew that the love of Christ had not prompted their offering; and all feared that their deceitful and wicked hearts would lead them to be proud of what they had done.

'We will pray,' said Miss Drummond, 'that Christ will forgive the sin that stains our best deeds, and that He will, day by day, more and more thoroughly purify the wishes, and thoughts, and motives of our hearts.'

ANON   *Nellie Grey*

Not Really *Stupid*

'Think again, Arthur. Is there nothing else you would like to come to London for? No new and curious machines? No Polytechnic Institution? No Panoramas and Dioramas of foreign places? No lectures to hear on chemistry and mechanics? No learned and clever masters to teach you? No shops, where you can buy books and mathematical instruments, and all things wanted for boys who mean to be cultivated and useful men, as well as first-rate engineers? Is there nothing but dirt and noise in London? Eh! Arthur?'

'Why you see, mamma,' began Arthur, crossing one little leg over the other, in an argumentative manner, while both hands (the top in one) disappeared in the pockets of his trousers. 'You see, mamma, I was thinking just then, how very nice it would be to live in the country, and so I forgot all about the useful things there are in London. That is just my way. It is

Off to school

very stupid of me, Fanny says. No, not *stupid*, she did not say *stupid*, because that would have been unkind; but very slow and dull, not to be able to consider two things at once. Fanny says it makes me *unfair;* and the other day papa was talking about some one who could not see two sides to a question, and he said that his judgment was worth nothing. Now, mamma that is like me. I have been wanting to speak to you about this. Fanny thinks that it is only because I am a little boy; and that when I am grown up, I shall be almost as sensible as you and papa, and nobody will say my judgment is worth nothing.

Now, I think, and it makes me so miserable, mamma,' here his little face was contracted slightly, and tears came into his honest blue eyes, – 'I am very much afraid that I was born rather stupid, and shall never be clever, and understand things rightly and quickly, as Fanny does. I should like to know what you think about it, mamma.'

Fanny jumped up, and threw her arms round her brother's neck, and kissed him, at the end of this speech, which was a long speech for Arthur, who was by no means a talkative boy. Mrs Reynolds knew by his looks, and by what he had said, that

Playing truant

his thoughts must have been much occupied with this subject; and although she felt very much inclined to kiss him too, and tell him he was quite clever enough for her to love him and listen to him at all times, yet she thought it would be best to try and satisfy his mind on the matter. So she looked quite grave, and said:

'I will tell you what I think, Arthur. You are only ten years old; and at that age the portion of your mind, called the reasoning power, is not developed, that is grown up. Things that are very plain and simple, you can understand; things that are not plain and simple you cannot understand. But if you continue strong and healthy in body, and strive to learn all the useful things that are taught you, and persevere in your present desire to be true and just, you will, by degrees, become a sensible fellow; and, in due time, a man, upon whose reasoning and judgment most people will rely – I for one.'

'You, mamma? You are so clever.'

'Yes, Arthur. It would not be very clever in me, you know, not to value the judgment of a well-informed, sensible man, because he was once my little sonny.' Here his mother drew him to her, and kissed his relaxing forehead.

'But am I not very slow in understanding, mamma? – Fanny learns and understands everything in a moment.'

'Yes, Arthur, my dear, you are rather slow at present; but you will not always be slow, I think. You must not think yourself stupid, because you cannot learn as fast as your sister. Remember, she is a year older than you, and that she is a girl. I do not know why God has made it so, but little girls generally learn much faster and better than little boys; but, when they are older, about seventeen or eighteen, boys learn more, and faster than girls, and much more difficult things. So if you wait patiently, you will do better than Fanny in a great many things.

'If I can only do half as well, mamma,' said Arthur beginning to take courage. 'I am so glad you think I am not really *stupid*,' and he kissed his mother affectionately.

'He need not make himself miserable about that – need he, mamma?' inquired Fanny, with a sweet-loving smile. 'He fears he shall be a silly, useless man, just because he cannot work a sum all right, at first, and spell long words, like *concatenation*.'

MISS WINNARD   *Fanny and Arthur*

Watching the Blood Flow

'Have you any objection to my being in the room, mamma,' said Harry; 'I should like to see an experiment upon a vein.'

'Not the least, provided you make your observations in silence. I shall be very willing to answer any inquiries afterwards; but, you know, it would be unreasonable to trouble Mr Sound with a little boy's questions, since he cannot be supposed to feel any particular interest in your improvement.' Almost as soon as Mrs Beaufoy had done speaking, the surgeon was announced; and Harry, silently taking his station beside his mother's chair, resolved to fulfil his part of the compact.

When the bright lancet approached the arm, his eyes were involuntarily averted; but he recovered himself in a moment, and beheld the blood flow with commendable philosophy.

When the surgeon thought the quantity taken was sufficient, he pressed his thumb upon Mrs Beaufoy's arm, about an inch *below* the orifice; and the blood, which before was flowing in a full stream, instantly stopped. Many boys would have failed to observe this; but Harry thought it the most curious part of the whole operation.

The arm was soon bound up, the surgeon took his leave, and Mrs Beaufoy, lying down on the sofa, desired Harry to come and sit beside her. 'Well, my dear,' said she, 'did you clearly understand this experiment on a vein?'

'Not quite, mamma. I do not know why Mr Sound tied that ugly red bandage round the upper part of your arm: it was so tight, that it must have hurt you.'

'It certainly caused an unpleasant sensation; but it was necessary, in order to prevent the blood in the arm from returning to the heart. You saw that Mr Sound did not attempt to make the incision till the vein, having received a quantity of blood from the arteries, appeared full and prominent: it would not have filled in that manner, if the bandage had not prevented the escape of the blood. But did you observe how he stopped the bleeding?'

'Yes, mamma; to be sure I did. It was the very reverse of papa's experiment on the artery: that was stopped by pressure *above*, the vein by pressure *below;* and this is a real proof that the blood runs in opposite directions through the veins and arteries: nothing could be plainer; and I only wish that I could see the action of the heart and its valves!'

'Now I feel very differently,' replied his mother. 'I regard the concealment of our internal organisation as one of the benevolent arrangements of Providence. Were it possible to view, through the skin, the whole of this complicated mechanism, the sight would completely frighten us. How should we dare to move, or stir a step, if we actually *saw* the heart pumping, the blood circulating, the lungs blowing, the tendons pulling, and all the intricate assemblage of fibres, tubes, valves, currents, pivots, and hinges, that sustain our frail existence! It is kindly and wisely ordered that these things should be hidden from our view.'

MARIA HACK   *Harry Beaufoy*, 1845

Don't Trust Popery

'Some people say that Popery has changed its character, and that cruelty is no longer practised, but if they knew their own hearts better they would talk more wisely. Good men have been destroyed by papists on the charge of having "relapsed into heresy," Is there no such thing possible as papists relapsing into cruelty? Do we not know that the heart remains the same till God changes it? And have we not read in Holy Scriptures that the dog will return to his vomit, and the sow to her wallowing in the mire? When a snake that has been scotched, or injured, recovers its strength, does it not again use its poisoned fangs? When a wounded tiger survives, does it not once more spring on its prey? Why, then, may not Popery, when it has the power, do what it did in former times?'

'I understand by what you say, that we ought not to trust Popery.'

'Indeed we ought not to trust it. It may possibly be the case, Robert, that what I have lately read and heard of the cruel sufferings of martyrs, and of the bitterness of their oppressors, may have made me more quick in my feelings on this subject, than I should otherwise have been; but it seems to me, that so long as there is a probability, I had almost said possibility, of these cruel burnings being again practised, it is a duty to keep alive the remembrance of them from one generation to another, even to the end of the world.'

'I shall not soon forget what you have told me of the martyrs, and of that cruel man Bonner.'

ANON   *Footprints of Popery*

The Morning Ride.

Ida's Education

'And what is the true enticement?'

'Usefulness.'

'But you would not make a woman *merely* useful?' persisted Mr Leverton.

'No – I would make her *greatly* useful. I consider accomplishments to be so as well as knowledge. Even in the formation of a flower, the Almighty has made the more beautiful parts essential to its value. The gaudy leaves of the tulip protect the germ from injury. On the same principle I would have every woman educated rather to form a valuable whole, than a brilliant part.'

'I have heard some very clever persons say, that education was always the effect of circumstances.'

'More shame for the parents who permit it to be so!' replied the lady.

'I, too, have often heard the observation; but *never* from those who had been cared for in their youth. I am willing to admit that strong minds are capable of great exertions, and frequently educate themselves; yet they always remind me of a garden, where some glorious flowers are cherished with peculiar care, but where you are perpetually annoyed by disagreeable weeds, that increase, multiply, and mar the beauty of the parterre. Nevertheless, granting that strong minds perform great things, what is to become of the weak ones? – They are not less valuable in the sight of the Creator because of their weakness, though, if neglected in their youth, they too often become wicked. But I am betrayed into the error of speaking a homily, where I only intended to make a reply. The young ladies will expect us to lead the way to their early supper, and — '

'We shall have plenty of time to talk over dear Ida's education,' interrupted her father, as he conducted the lady to the supper-room.

MRS S. C. HALL   *The Juvenile Budget*, 1846

'Smoke Not'

BY A WORKING MAN

Two schoolfellows, of equal age,
Were 'prenticed in one day;
The one was studiously inclined,
The other boy was gay.

The pocket-money each received
Was just the same amount;
And how they both expended it,
I briefly shall recount.

While George was smoking his cigars,
And sauntering about,
With youths as idle as himself,
Shutting all knowledge out;

At the Mechanics' Institute,
And with his books at home,
Tom wisely spent his leisure hours,
Nor cared the streets to roam.

One eve, when their apprenticeship
Had nearly passed away,
George at his friend Tom's lodgings called
An hour or two to stay.

He entered smoking his cigar,
Ill-mannerly enough,
And staring round the room, he blew
A most portentous puff.

'Why, Tom!' he cried, with much surprise,
'Is your old uncle dead?
And left you cash to buy those books
That round the walls are spread?'

'Oh no,' said Tom, 'I bought those books
With what my friends allowed.
Had you not smoked away your cash,
You might the same have showed!'

'Why, my Havannahs only cost
Me threepence every day!'
'Just so,' said Tom, 'you've only smoked
A library away!

'Now reckon up threepence a day
For seven long years to come!
And you will find that it will count
A very handsome sum!'

'Why, that,' said George, with humbled look,
'Full THIRTY POUNDS would be;
How foolishly I've smoked away
A handsome library.'

WILLIAM MARTIN (Ed.)   *Peter Parley's Annual*, 1866

Missionary Corner

Dear Mr Editor,
I like your 'Missionary Corner' very much, and I want to do something for those poor black boys. It said in February that it costs £7 to keep a boy at the Mission for a year. I want to know whether the boys and girls who read MY SUNDAY FRIEND can't collect £7 a year and send it to you to keep a black slave-boy at the school, and teach him about Jesus Christ. I dare say we could, if we tried. Perhaps we could keep *two* boys there. So I send you two shillings from my sister Ethel and me, and I hope a lot more boys and girls will do it.
So I remain

Your affectionate Sunday Friend,
John William B –
(Aged 11)

(What do our Sunday Friends say? The Editor thinks we might easily do as our capital little friend suggests, and pay for the maintenance of a boy at the Zanzibar Mission School. Seven pounds a year is not much among so many. We got more than that last year for the Day in the Country. Shall we try?)

REV H. C. SHUTTLEWORTH (Ed.)   *My Sunday Friend*,
May 1878

This Little Pig - in Swahili

It is very sad to see the children when they are first brought to the Mission school. All of them are in want, many are sick, and some insane from the cruel treatment they have received from the slave dealers. Their home was, perhaps, 500 miles away inland, near the great Lake Nyassa. One night, just as they had fallen comfortably asleep, they had been awakened by a crackling of flames and stifling smoke, and rushing out of their little hut, which being built of split bamboo canes and thatched with long grass looked like a big beehive, they were seized by the Arabs or some neighbour who had a grudge against their father, and carried away from father and mother, from sister and brother, away they knew not whither. Next morning they were tied together, one behind the other, in a long string, and to prevent their running away there was fastened a long slave stick round their necks, something like a hay-fork, with its prongs pressing on each side, and fastened together under the throat with a block of wood. And so they had to walk on, up-hill and down-hill; if anyone flagged, there was the whip to urge him on; if any sank down faint, there he was left to die, or killed because he could not rise. Men have been known ere this to take a little baby from its mother's arms, and dash its brains out against the nearest tree, because she was weak and weary. No wonder that when the party reach the coast five out of every eight that started have died by the way, and that Miss Allen, the kind lady who is in charge of the hospital at Zanzibar, says:

'Their early troubles have made these little ones so preter-naturally solemn. When they first come, I have hard work to get a smile from them. I try Bo-peep and various childish games to get a laugh out of them. I have a number of little ones in the hospital just now from Mbroczi, most of them with a dreadful African skin disease. Mr Capel says it is from the quantities of unripe mangoes they have lately been eating.

'The other day, almost in despair, I at last tried, 'This Pig went to Market,' etc., a new and original version in Swahili, for their benefit. The first child looked very solemn over it until I came to 'Wee, wee, give me some-ee,' when I was rewarded by the applause of childish laughter, and I had one row of little black fingers after another held up for the per-formance.'

R.M.H.

REV H. C. SHUTTLEWORTH (Ed.) *My Sunday Friend*, July 1878

Above: Moth, Nest, Ox and Pig
Part of a picture alphabet from *The Little Learner's*
Toy Book
Right: An early French lesson from *The Pictorial*
Word Book

An arm-chair.
Un fauteuil.

A bed.
Un lit.

A chest of drawers
Une commode.

A secretary.
Un secrétaire.

A stool.
Un tabouret.

A candlestick.
Un chandelier.

A watch.
Une montre.

A piano.
Un piano.

A bed-room.
Une chambre à coucher.

A book-case.
Une bibliothèque.

A chair.
Une chaise.

A cradle.
Un berceau.

A clock.
Une pendule.

A looking-glass.
Une glace.

A lustre.
Un lustre.

Curtains.
Des rideaux.

A stove.
Un poêle.

A lamp.
Une lampe.

A carpet.
Un tapis.

A picture.
Un tableau

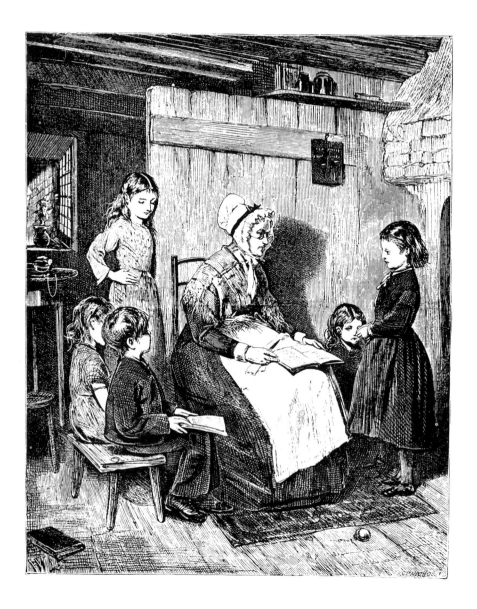

The Village Schoolmistress

In every village marked with little spire,
Embowered in trees, and hardly known to fame,
There dwells, in lowly cot, and mean attire,
A matron old, whom we schoolmistress name;
Her cap, far whiter than the driven snow,
Emblem right meet of decency does yield;
Her apron neatly trimmed, as blue, I trow,
As is the harebell that adorns the field.

ANON   Pictures For our Pets

Useful and Agreeable Occupations

While they were enjoying the view, they heard a bell ring; and looking round, saw a crowd of children flocking towards a neat stone building.

'The windows of that building are larger and handsomer than those of a cottage,' observed Godfrey; 'I should think it is a school-house, and that those children are some of the scholars.'

'Yes,' said Mrs Campbell; 'it is the school-house that was built some years ago, for the children of the fishermen and cottagers of Hastings. We will ask the mistress to allow us to go in; I like to see young people engaged in useful and agreeable occupations.'

Mrs Campbell spoke to the school-mistress, who readily permitted her and the boys to see the school. The school-room was large, airy, and convenient. The cleanliness of the well boarded floor, the smooth white walls, ornamented with coloured views of different countries, and large prints of animals, the bright faced clock, and the polished fire-place, with a large nosegay in the grate, gave a cheerful gay look to the scene, which was very agreeable to the eye. Two elder girls stood at a table, giving out slates and writing-books, while a third unlocked a cupboard, and distributed needle-work. On each side of the fire-place were a few shelves for those books which were employed in instructing the children; and a small book-case displayed through its glass doors a number of entertaining and amusing books, which were lent to the young people to read, as rewards for diligence and good conduct. The school-mistress assured Mrs Campbell that these books were much valued. She also gave Mrs Campbell many particulars about the school. Each child, she said, paid threepence a week, and she showed several specimens of their needle-work, writing, etc. The children chiefly worked for their parents; and great, she said was the delight of the little ones when they were first able to make a shirt for a father or a brother. She pointed to one little girl, who looked particularly bright and happy, and who was occupied in rubbing out the lines from a sheet of paper, on which she had written a letter to an aunt in London. The mistress said that the little girl had employed the usual play hour for that purpose, and the letter now only required to be folded up and directed.

As Mrs Campbell left the school-house with the boys, both of them expressed the pleasure this hasty visit had given them. 'How well some of the little girls read and wrote!' exclaimed Arthur.

'And how comfortable they all looked in their pleasant room!' said Godfrey.

'Yes,' said Mrs Campbell; 'those children possess advantages and conveniences of which the chiefs and warriors who built and defended yonder old castle, were quite ignorant. *They* could not amuse themselves with a book, nor write letters to their absent friends.'

'Oh, mamma, surely chiefs and warriors could read,' said Godfrey.

'Grown up people not know how to read and write!' exclaimed Arthur; 'you must be joking, mamma.'

ANON   The Parent's Cabinet, 1859

Little Ears

The poor mother who pays twopence a-day to have her child taken care of, while she labours to earn its daily bread, performs her duty to the extent of her knowledge, not to the extent of her feelings; for, amid all her toils, her heart yearns towards her offspring, and now, since the establishment of infant schools, she can leave it in comparative safety. But I address you, well-born, accomplished, if not well-educated women; rich in the good things of this world; rich in the gifts that many covet, of children born to perpetuate your name, your rank. If by any neglect of yours – if, by an unpardonable negligence, your children receive wrong and dangerous *first* impressions, believe me you ensure to yourselves anxious maturity, neglected old age, and the reproaches of your own conscience. I must not be told of 'the claims of society,' of 'engagements,' of other duties; a well-arranged *ménage* will provide for all; and, if you are careful yourself, your governess, your nurse, will become careful also: you may soon discover, at all events, whether such is or is not the case . . . I can, therefore, only entreat *both* parents to watch their words in the presence of their children, and to bear in mind that 'little ears' have a decided propensity for remembering what they ought not to remember.

MRS S. C. HALL   The Juvenile Budget, 1846

The Old Dame School

Under the master the boys were taught to read and spell, to write and cipher, and to be kind and courteous to one another. In addition to this, certain hours in the week were set apart for instruction in geography, history, and natural history, or the science which treats of living creatures. To help the children in these studies, the walls of the larger room, where the boys were taught, were hung with large maps of all parts of the world, with pictures of scenes and events of importance in the history of our own country, and with large coloured sheets, in which were portrayed not only the birds and animals common in England, but numbers of the savage beasts found in foreign countries, and numbers more of the great monsters found in the sea. The walls of the class-room, too, in which a Bible-class, formed of the elder boys and girls, met once a

The ten o'clock scholar

week, were almost covered over with coloured prints of subjects taken from the Old and New Testament. These maps and pictures gave the inside of the schoolhouse a very cheerful and lively appearance; but, what was far better than that, they were a source of continual interest and instruction to the children, who not only learned from them by the explanations of the master and mistress, but got knowledge from each other by talking about them.

When John Godwin, on calling on Mr Thompson to inquire about placing his children at school, first saw the inside of the place, and what was going on there, he was fairly struck with wonder. He had never seen anything of that sort before, for in that day there were very few village schools which were half so well supplied with the means of instruction as village schools are now. John called to mind the old dame-school at Bolton, to which his good mother had sent him as soon as he was old enough to toddle along the road by himself. He remembered the poor old woman who kept it; how she left the children, sometimes by the hour together, to scrub her room, or to boil her pot for dinner; how at others she sat fast asleep over her knitting until she was woke up by the noise and squabbling of the boys and girls; he remembered her long birch rod, and the fear he had of it; he seemed to see again the one small 'Reading Made Easy,' which he had thumbed into dog's-ears long before he had mastered words of one syllable; and when he called these old days up to view, he wondered how it was that he had ever learned to read at all. Contrasting the advantages which were offered to his children with the scanty means of education which he had enjoyed himself, Godwin, like a sensible man, determined that his boys and girls should reap the benefit of the school as far as possible, and get all the learning it was in his power to provide for them. . . .

During six months in the year, when the days were short, Mr Thompson opened the school of an evening, for the benefit of such of the lads and young men of the neighbourhood whose education had been neglected, or who desired further to improve themselves. To this evening school Sam Godwin, who worked at the farm whenever he could get employed, went regularly five nights a week all through the winter, his father consenting that he should set apart a portion of his earnings to pay the weekly money. Thus, if he lost time by being absent from school during the hay-making, and harvest, and other

'Will you come to my
Sunday School?'

busy seasons at the farm, he made up for it by his evening
studies.

It was a part of the schoolmistress's plan, in which she was
encouraged by most of the ladies and respectable housekeepers
of the neighbourhood, to instruct such of the girls as were
intended for service in the proper methods of doing domestic
work. This she did by finding them employment in her own
house after school hours and overlooking what they did. Some
of the parents of the girls were silly enough to object to this,
and to forbid their daughters from remaining after school hours
for any such purpose. These over-wise mothers could only look
at the subject from a selfish point of view: they imagined that
the schoolmistress wanted their children to do her work, and
they could not see how important it is that a young girl who is
to get her living by her work, should be taught from the beginning to do her work in the best manner.

ANON *The Cottage at the Firs*

Friend or Tyrant?

'What have they been doing to you, Steenie, my lad?' said a masculine-looking woman, to her son, a boy about eleven years of age, who came towards her sniffing and polishing his dirty cheeks with his jacket sleeve.

'Never mind,' said the boy, pushing past her and seating himself near the door.

'Who has been ill-treating you, I say?' the woman persisted. 'Was it that new school-master?'

The boy began to cry again, and said, 'Yes.'

'Mr Barnard had better mind what he's about,' said the woman. 'I'll go right up to the school, and tell him so.'

'Oh no, mother! it don't signify,' said Stephen.

'But it does signify,' she answered. 'I am not going to have you knocked about to please him. What was it for?'

'I don't know – at least, I don't want to make no fuss about it.'

'Come along with me. I'll go up to the school-master straight away, and tell him a bit of my mind. Poor people's children are made of flesh and blood, and has feelings like other folks, and he ought to know it.'

The rebuke

'What's the good?' he continued, as his mother seized him by the hand, and tried to drag him along with her. 'I won't go – there!'

Mrs Alloway yielded to the boy as she usually did, and went on alone towards the school-house. 'He is the most forgiving child I ever saw,' she said to herself; 'and that makes it so much worse when any one ill-treats him.'

Mr Barnard was engaged with one of the pupil-teachers, after school-hours, when suddenly the door was flung open, and an angry woman without a bonnet, and with her hair straggling wildly about her cheeks, entered the room, and demanded, 'What have you been hitting my boy for?'

'Your boy, Mrs Alloway? In the first place, he played truant; and then, to excuse himself, told me a falsehood.'

'Well, and if he did, what right had you to punish him like that?'

'It was a very moderate punishment; has he complained?'

'No; I can't say that he did, he's too forgiving; but that's no excuse for you. You ought to have talked to him if he did wrong, and told him.'

'Of course, Mrs Alloway, I did that also. I should be very glad indeed if reproof alone would do, without the rod. I would never punish a child if I could help it. The pain your boy suffered, and the quiet talk I have had with him, will, I hope, together, have a good effect upon him, if you will only deal prudently with him at home. He is very well disposed, and does not want sense; but is idle, and too ready to be led away by others older than himself. If you would talk to him seriously, and give him some good advice, I have no doubt you would soon find him more obedient, and you would have more comfort in him as he grows up.'

'Now, is it not mortifying?' said Mr Barnard, turning to the pupil-teacher. 'That boy Alloway will be ruined in spite of all I can do for him. His father drinks, and neglects him; and his mother is foolish, and spoils him. The boy has good feelings, and was quite penitent when he left this room; but he is taught to think himself ill-used, and to look upon me as a tyrant, instead of a friend. I dare say he will not come to school at all to-morrow; and if he does, it will be only to sulk and be idle. How is it possible for me to do him any good under such circumstances?'

ANON *Steenie Alloway's Adventures*

Black Monday

I cannot think what makes school-masters and school-mistresses so fond of keeping school; they don't always look so very pleasant at their work, and yet to see how very kindly they treat us when we come, and how glad they are to see us, and look so cheerful, and give such hearty shakes of the hands, and such huggings, and make so many tender enquiries about 'Ma' and 'Pa.' What good wonderful people school-masters and school-mistresses must be, and are; and then they love us so, that when they tickle us, as they call it, it is to make us smart they say; and they do make us smart! It is for our good, we know that. But the best of it is to see how nicely they help us in our books, particularly our writing-books; and how nicely they paint up our letters and correct the 'broad downs' and the 'fine ups,' and put all our figures to rights for us, and compose, too, such beautiful holiday letters, and give us so many chances. They are a kind, good-hearted race of 'beings,' as Aunt Crawfish calls them. And so school is a happy place, after all, and I don't care so much for BLACK MONDAY when it does come: there is good fun at school as well as at home – think of bolstering and all that. But the best thing after all, is to think of the 'lessons,' the 'tasks' and the 'duties,' – so here's for mathematical diversion, Greek hexameters, and Latin verse, and all the rest of it. I dont mind! If I must, I must! Make me happy then 'Pedagogicus' and hold out the open arms of your good nature, and I will leap into them with right good will.

So, hurray for 'Hanwell College,' and all other noble institutions, where boys are treated so kindly as to make them as glad to get back to school, as they were to go home for their holidays.

WILLIAM MARTIN (Ed.)   *Peter Parley's Annual*, 1858

According to The Girl's Own Book, '*this play should be used with caution*'

144

The School Treat

The tables long with clean white cloths,
And buns and cakes, were spread;
The room was dressed with flowers, and flags
Were waving overhead.

And boys and girls came thronging round,
All washed and combed and neat –
They were the children of the school,
And this their yearly treat.

And very pleasant 'twas to see
Each happy, shining face,
And hear their voices when they stood
And sang their pretty grace.

And then the busy teachers went
Among them, here and there,
With tea, and cakes, and buns, till all
Had plenty, and to spare.

And while we watched that active band,
How glad we felt to see
Two happy little children, kind,
Handing the mugs of tea.

Their smiling faces seemed to say,
As loud as words, I'm sure,
'Oh, what a pleasant thing it is
To feed the hungry poor.'

'Ah!' thought I, 'when the busy scenes
Of life shall be no more,
And those two little girls shall stand
Upon the unknown shore –

'May Fanny and may Alice find
These words their joy to be,
"Ye did it to the least of these,'"
And therefore unto me.'

JOSEPHINE Jottings For Juveniles, 1862

Remember the Sabbath

This kind governess, . . . is anxious to make her little pupils love Sunday, and she tries to make it the brightest day of all the seven. She takes them to one Service; and then, in the afternoon, they all go with her to the Infant School, which is a great amusement to them. She has a class herself, and these three stand by her, and answer the questions when the little village children cannot. Then they come home, and she teaches them to sing hymns, so that they may be able to lead the little ones in school – they are delighted to do this. Then they have tea and are dressed to go down to dessert with papa and mamma – a treat reserved only for Sundays; and they go into the drawing-room afterwards, when papa tells them a story and mamma sings to them; and then, children and all, sing an evening hymn, and go to bed, after a quiet, happy day, in which all have tried to 'keep Christ's holy day in the happiest, fittest way.'

ANON *Children's Sunday Album*

Airs and Graces

Mr Moffat's father had been a tallow-chandler, and Mrs Moffat's papa made his money by keeping wine vaults in London. Retiring to Devonshire with a moderate fortune made by the industry of their parents, they would have been res-pected by persons of their own sphere of life as well as by their superiors, had they conducted themselves as sensible people. But they had an idea that a little independence put them upon a level with that class of persons called the gentry of the neighbourhood; and all the desire of Mr and Mrs Moffat was to be considered genteel, and to be on visiting terms with Mrs Captain Green or Mr Major Brown, or to take tea occasionally with the second cousin of the Recorder of Exeter, or to dine with the son-in-law of one of the town council. Mr Moffat was proud to acknowledge that he had breakfasted with a lord at such and such a place, and dined with a marquis at another; never letting out the secret that these breakfastings and dinings were public ones, at which anybody dined or break-fasted who could pay a guinea for it.
Master Moffat was therefore placed at school with due direc-

tions from his mamma to the schoolmaster that he should be kept from mixing with his inferiors – that he should be taught to be a perfect gentleman – that he should wear silk stockings and white gloves, sport an eye-glass and carry a riding-whip. The monthly carriage visit was to put the finishing stamp upon the whole, and to strike dignity into the eyes and hearts of the poor plebeian boys who could not afford to pay the extra five pounds a year as parlour boarders.

The schoolmaster, Mr Wellsop, was one of that class of teachers who pretend to know a great deal, but know nothing. He had a certain smattering of Latin and Greek, which he dignified with the high name of classical attainments. He could not ascertain what was two-thirds of three-fourths of a plum-pudding without being bothered, and yet called himself a professor of mathematics. In short, he was what is called an empiric or quack, and as such he assumed most consequential airs and graces, put on a pompous phraseology in his common speech, and assumed a ha-haw inarticulate drawl. He used to talk most largely of his carriage pupils – although he had but one, and of his connections, whom nobody knew anything of – not even himself.

Under all these circumstances it is not to be wondered at that the 'parlour boarders' were in a fair way of being adepts at all kinds of mischief, and that they were by no means likely to get into any very considerable penalties on account of it; for

Mr Wellsop was not the man to lose sight of his own interest by so checking his pupils as to lose them, and therefore very quietly let them have their own way as much as possible, and perhaps a little more.

There was one peculiarity, if it can be so called, of these young gentlemen which was well calculated to show their vulgar origin. They were always munching, – always had something between their teeth; whether in school or out of school, in bed or out of it, still their mouths were in the action of chewing. At one time nuts, at another cakes; bull's eyes, brandy balls, elecampane, liquorice, lozenges, drops, jujubes, and above all things were they fond of apples; and if anything could increase the delight with which they munched them, or could add to their flavour, it was the consciousness of having *stolen* them.

PETER PARLEY   *The Hatchups*, 1858

'You Don't Know Your Letters?'

Her timid knock at the heavy oaken door of the school-room was at first unheard, owing to the busy hum of voices within. She ventured at length upon a louder knock, and then the door opened a little way, and a girl peeped out.

'Oh, Miss Katherine, here's a new girl!' and in a minute a young lady, with a fair and pleasant face, stood in the doorway.

Elsie could see the school now, as the door was opened wide. She saw what appeared to her to be an enormous number of girls, most of them diligently at work, with several ladies moving about amongst them. And opposite her, on the school-room wall, was a large picture that riveted her attention in a moment. It was the 'Good Shepherd,' about whom her mother had told her something, and Mr Johnson had told her more. She could not take her eyes off the picture. Miss Katherine was obliged to repeat her question, 'Do you want to be taken into this school?' twice before Elsie collected her scattered thoughts sufficiently to answer her. 'Yes, if you please, miss; but I don't know anything.'

'That doesn't matter, if you are clean and will behave well,' was the reply. 'You don't know your letters? Then you must go into this class,' – pointing to a class not far from the door, –

The Lesson.

'where there are girls as old as you are who don't know any-thing. You will soon get on if you try. Here, Mary, is another pupil for you.' Miss Katherine addressed a lady rather younger, but so like herself, that Elsie thought they were sisters.

The girls in the class appeared to be nearly as untaught and ignorant as she was, and far less eager to learn. Before the evening was half over, Elsie, although sufficiently well used to the general behaviour of girls of her kind, began to wonder greatly how they could be so troublesome in that room, which seemed to her to have something holy about it, and to the kind, gentle girl, who was teaching them. She was sitting by a great, ungainly-looking creature, not very unlike the Elsie of three weeks ago in dress and general appearance. But far from sharing Elsie's desire for instruction, she tormented the poor new-comer at every opportunity, and put every hindrance she could think of in the way of her learning. All was not to be so delightful and smooth at the school as Elsie had fondly imagined. Before eight o'clock, her temper, which she was unaccustomed, when under any considerable provocation, to control, got the better of her, and, to her great dismay, she found herself put out of the class as a punishment for striking Julia Brown, her tormentor. The blow descended upon Julia Brown in consequence of that amiable young person having effaced, with one good rub of her hand, all the letters on poor Elsie's slate, which she had been half-an-hour forming with great care and toil.

Elsie cried bitterly, but did not tell of Julia Brown, and the teacher only heard Julia's shriek on receiving the blow.

A.R.N. *Little Seymour Street; or, Elsie Feltham*

The Flush of Triumph

Poor boys have the feelings of rich boys. The Latins and Greeks of the 'College' schools, and the would-be first wranglers in mathematics, who are looking out to be 'freshmen' at Oxford, or 'sophs' at Cambridge, have not finer feelings than the poor lads whose only ambition it is to show the excellence of their 'pot-hooks and hangers.' They have the noble ambition of being perfect in the three R's – Reading, Riting, and Rithmetic. Some say that charity boys are nothing but *vulgar fractions*, and scorn them and their Christmas pieces; but there are those of the right sort who look upon their performances with a kindly eye.

And so in the Christmas holidays we see the Grammar School boys, and the boys of the National Schools, all eagerly striving for the honour of being the best boy – Dux. No, there are no 'Dux' in charity schools, although there may be a few geese to be plucked. Who is the best boy is the great inquiry of the parish notables; perhaps the squire, may be the parson, may be the squire's wife, or the parson's wife, and what is almost as good, the farmer and his noble house-wife: and these sit in grand state, and hear the boys read the parable of the Good Samaritan, and see the grand caligraphy of a Christmas piece, 'Mend your manners,' emblazoned, and showing the heraldry

Picture teaching – and a social lesson

of 'coloured prints,' glorious with red and yellow.

It is a pleasant sight to see; but even more pleasant is it to watch the countenance of the youngster when a compeer makes a blunder in his spelling, or when his own sum comes right almost of its own accord. The flush of triumph on his cheek is like the rosy ray of the golden dawn, and the smile of satisfaction from the parson and the parson's lady, and the squire and squire's lady, and the farmer and the farmer's *wife*, are all of them worthy of contemplation.

When the examination is ended, and the prizes awarded, what various feelings agitate the breasts of the boys as they go to their homes. The successful ones burning with anxiety to show their parents the fruits of their good conduct; and of the unsuccessful – what can we say of them – only to hope they mentally resolve to work harder, and be more attentive during the next year, and strive to win not only a prize, but what is better still, the approving smile of their friends.

Thanks, then, to those who take to the poor boys – to the 'charity brats,' as they are called. Their purpose is a worthy and congenial one at Christmas-time, and with it the 'festival' that follows, and is not unworthy of Him who blessed little children, and turned the water into wine – who is ever anxious that the young should turn to Him. He is no particular respecter of 'clever boys,' or 'diligent boys,' or 'heroic boys,' but gives the crown of His smile to 'good boys,' such as partake of His love, and who are striving to do their duty both to God and man.

WILLIAM MARTIN (Ed.)   *Peter Parley's Annual*, 1866

God's Ragged Scholars

The band of labourers now, though scant and small,
To see the *firstfruits* with delight begin;
A time will come, when in the sight of all,
The glorious *harvest* shall be gathered in:
And thousands then in heaven's unclouded calm
Shall bow to Him who doth all nations rule;
Strike the sweet harp, and wave the victor's palm,
And bless the Saviour for the 'Ragged School.'

ANON   *Pictures For Our Pets*

REQUIRED *the name and description*
ANSWER *Shenstone, a standard English poet*

The Young Carver

To find Martin you must, in imagination, follow me into the heart of London. Leaving the great thoroughfares, we turn up a by-street, and pause before a large pile of building. We enter, and find ourselves in a room long, wide, and lofty, and capable of holding some two or three hundreds of persons. It is evening, and the place is bright with many gas-lights. The room has plainly been built for use, not for show; for the walls would be bare and unsightly were they not, in most parts, covered with numberless plaster casts – reproductions of many of the most beautiful works of fine or of ornamental art that ancient or modern times have produced. This place is a Government School of Art, and the one of which my friend Mr Burrow is the head-master.

Across the greater part of the room are ranges of seats, upon which many boys and some young men are sitting whilst they are drawing from plaster casts or from lithographs which are placed in front of them. All appear to be deeply interested and happy in their pleasant work; and you scarcely hear a word spoken, except by the teachers, who are moving from place to place; pointing out defects, and giving instructions. This is the elementary school, where the students receive their earlier instruction in drawing. We shall not find Martin here. He has long ago passed through this part of the course of instruction, with much satisfaction to his teachers and credit to himself.

To find Martin Farley we must pass beyond a wooden partition which screens off one end of the room. This is the 'Antique School,' and to be privileged to work in it is a great object of ambition with the students on the outer side of the screen. Scattered about it stand a number of full-sized casts from the most famous antique statues – the master-pieces of ancient Greece and Rome; and from these the students – mostly young men, or youths approaching manhood – are at work. The greater number are standing at their easels making elaborate drawings in chalk, but some few are modelling from the statues in clay; and among the latter is our friend Martin. . . . The evening seems to have been too short for Martin when the bell rings, and the gas is turned down, and his precious model has to be wrapped up in wet cloths for the night; but for all that, he will limp home to his humble lodgings with a light and merry heart, and dream of his model till morning. Through the day, to-morrow, he will not be a whit less happy whilst he chips away at the fine stone pulpit which he is carving in the shop of Mr Spandril, the church-decorator; and evening will again find him at his delightful labours in the School of Art.

FRANK SCARLETT POTTER   *The Sexton's Grandsons*

Life's Prizes

The danger we now are to apprehend from new modes and methods is, that the great salient points of school instruction should be slurred over for the sake of cramming children with what they can't understand, and which would never be of any use to them if they did. In many schools the children are well up in a great variety of scientific and historical and philosophical jargon; but are at the same time very poor readers, very sad writers, and very sorry arthimeticians.

This won't do, and parents will find others out by-and-by; and as it frequently happens that I am allowed to say a word to parents as well as to children, I can't refrain now from giving a hint or two to them. Take care that your children are taught to read well, that they are enabled to write a good hand, and that they are well acquainted with the fundamental rules of arithmetic; these are essentials, and if they be neglected in early days, the neglect can rarely be remedied in after life.

The New Building, under the Terrace, co

Frontispiece of *A Visit to the Zoological Gardens*
(evidently a solemn occasion)

for the Lions, Tigers, and other similar Animals.

It is, as I said, a beautiful sight to be at a 'school examination' when the children are not put forth for 'display' and when they are not stuffed up with conceit and vanity. In a great village school that I went to see the other day the prizes were being distributed; there was the dear old clergyman, with a face on which was written, 'Glory to God in the highest, on earth peace, and good will towards men,' with his neat and amiable wife overflowing with the milk of human kindness, distributing the little marks of approbation to those around her. The children were quiet, meek, orderly and loving, and God's sunshine seemed to glow through them while they sung the evening hymn at the sweet close of a lovely midsummer day. The prizes we compete for in the school-room are many and various; but what are the prizes we should endeavour to win in the great contention of life? Not fame, nor wealth, nor popular applause – the true prizes of our hearts are to have acquired truth and loving kindness, contentment, honour and honesty, humility, and above all, christian charity; the heart that has acquired these, is indeed a prize in itself, and will be prized by our Father who is in heaven.

w.m. *The Birthday Gift*, 1861

GAMES &
PASTIMES

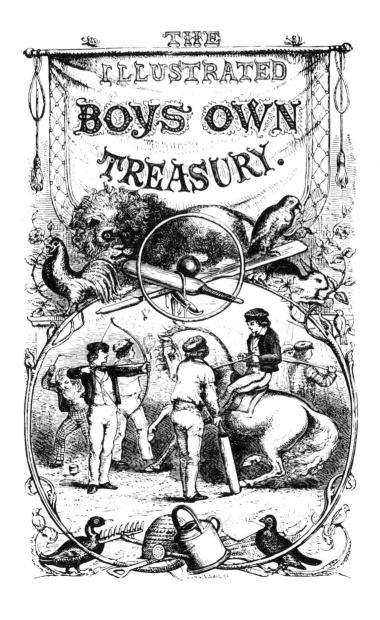

THE
ILLUSTRATED
BOYS OWN
TREASURY.

Adults injected their literalness and passion for scientific facts into what they thought were the proper pastimes for children. If an occupation was instructive, it won approval. If it could impress socially, and became an accomplishment, it was even more praiseworthy.

Playing the adult way, with all those tedious instructions, must have been hard work, like life itself. Sports sanctioned by Royalty and the Aristocracy soon became encouraged. Not only were they good for the physique, but they improved the character. This could be the only reconciliation to the doctrine that by playing a mere Game you were committing the sin of Wasting Time. You might even be tempted to gamble.

Girls, thanks to Miss Beale and Miss Buss, were about to be educated like their brothers. With the disappearance of the crinoline, their physical education looked like going the same way.

In suggestions for amusements, creativity and the realms of the imagination received relatively scant attention. Perhaps it was because the Aristocracy, who gave the lead in leisure, were hardly addicted to intellectual and aesthetically creative pursuits. Creativity was subordinate to technical skill, as little fingers were kept busy making holders, covers, samplers, bead-work cosies and every conceivable embellishment for the already over-ornate knick-knacks.

Since children had to have diversions, they had better be useful ones. High spirits and hilarity, yes. Rapture and ecstacy, never.

Out-of-Door Exercises

Walking, and other out-of-door exercises, cannot be too much recommended to young people. Even skating, driving hoop, and other boyish sports, may be practised to great advantage by little girls, provided they can be pursued within the inclosure of a garden, or court; in the street, they would, of course, be highly improper. It is true, such games are rather violent, and sometimes noisy; but they tend to form a vigorous constitution; and girls who are habitually lady-like, will never allow themselves to be rude and vulgar, even in play.

MRS CHILD   *The Girl's Own Book*, 1848

Calisthenics

This hard name is given to a gentler sort of gymnastics, suited to girls. The exercises have been very generally introduced into the schools in England, and are getting into favour in America. Many people think them dangerous, because they confound them with the ruder and more daring gymnastics of boys; but such exercises are selected as are free from danger; and it is believed that they tend to produce vigorous muscles, graceful motion, and symmetry of form.

CIRCULAR MOVEMENT OF THE ARMS

In this exercise, one arm, at first hanging by the side, is moved backward; it then passes up by the ear, and is brought down in front. The hand, which is kept folded, thus describes a circle from the shoulder.
This is first to be done with one arm, then with the other, and, lastly, with both together – slowly, steadily, and equably.

POINTING TO THE GROUND

The hands are first raised above the head, and then decline forward, the body bending; and the performer points the hands as low toward the ground as possible, but without bending the legs.

THE SPECTRE MARCH

The hands are to be placed on the hips, the thumbs turned back, and the performers, raising themselves on their toes, are then to move forward by a rapid succession of very small springs, keeping the whole frame as erect as possible.

THE DANCING STEP

The hands should be placed as before. A small hop is then to be made on the toes, with one foot, the other coming forward and repeating the hop; and the performer thus advances, by a hop and a step, with each foot alternately.

EXERCISES WITH THE WAND

The wand for this purpose should be light and smooth, but not of a nature to bend. It is first to be taken hold of near the extremities, by each hand, with the knuckles outward; then raised to the perpendicular position, the right hand being uppermost; the left then takes its place. This should be performed rapidly for some time.

The wand is to be raised above the head; it is then to be passed behind; and, finally, returned, into the first position of the wand, by a reverse progress of the arms.

The wand is to be held as before, except that the knuckles are

Calisthenics

turned behind; it is then to be raised parallel with the shoulders, each hand being turned alternately inward, so that the end of the wand passes between the fore-arm and the shoulder.
It is then to be lifted above the head and brought down behind. It is finally returned to the original position. These exercises should be repeated many times, till the pupil is very expert and rapid.

MRS CHILD The Girl's Own Book, 1848

Low Trickery

Keen chopping and changing of marbles, tops, or other kinds of playthings between boys, is very apt to give rise to fraud. The over-reaching of one another in bargains of this sort, with the love of pelf and self, is calculated to spoil the noble, free, and generous disposition that should belong to boyhood. The accumulation and hoarding of playthings is another very silly thing for boys to do, yet I have known boys with such accumulations of tops, buttons, marbles, and other toys, as to be quite ridiculous. Such boys are generally great screws, and grudge everybody the playthings they may happen to have. Such boys are likely to become old misers before they die.
A high-minded, generous boy will do none of these things. He will not only play fairly, but he will act liberally, and always be ready to lend any of his school or play-fellows his toys or playthings. In return for this noble conduct, those who borrow should be careful to return what they borrow, and be as ready to lend what they can conveniently spare.
Boys should avoid all contemptible shuffling, or low trickery, squeezing and pinching conduct. They should be open-hearted and sincere, generous and off-handed, and have a hatred for every species of sneaking meanness. In all their dealings with each other, whether in the school-room or playground, they should act towards each other with fairness. By so doing they will be a far deal more happy than they will by all the arts and

cunning which they may employ to suit their own crooked purposes. If there be one thing above another for which youth is to be pre-eminently distinguished, it is for its generous ardour, its generosity, and its sincerity. When these are wanting, the charm of boyhood is gone; and we are easily induced to look upon boys as great nuisances and pests, scarcely to be tolerated in their thoughtless pranks and senseless follies.

WILLIAM MARTIN (Ed.) *Peter Parley's Annual*, 1866

How to Play Football

This excellent game, after having been much neglected, has again attracted attention, and is now very popular. In some parts of England and Scotland it is annually played on Shrove Tuesday: notably in the town of Kingston-upon-Thames and the villages adjacent. Football is also deservedly a favourite game at Harrow, Eton, Rugby, Marlborough, Westminster, and other public schools. Simply described, Football is played in the following manner:

A match is made between two sets of players of equal numbers; a large ball made of light materials – a blown bladder, or an India-rubber ball, cased with leather, is the best – is placed within them, and the object of each party of players is to kick the ball across the goal of the other, and to prevent it from passing their own. The party across whose goal the ball is kicked loses the game. The game is commenced between the two goals, which are generally about a hundred yards asunder.

ANON *The Boy's Own Book*, 1878

A Sport Paramount

This truly English pastime, although long a favourite with the people of this country, never reached to a greater degree of popularity than it possesses at this time. It is a favourite with the peer and the peasant – the Socius Societas Artium and the schoolboy. Royalty has, heretofore, stood bat in hand at the popping-crease, surrounded by those youthful buds of nobility of which our nation has since been proud; and, strange though it may seem, yet it is no less strange than true – young matrons have played matches of Cricket against maidens, having husbands, brothers, and sweethearts for their spectators.

In many counties, Cricket is the universal pastime of the people; in others, it is rarely played, and in some, scarcely mentioned. The man of Devon, who deems all sports inferior to wrestling, and the inhabitant of Somerset, who doats upon the manly game of single stick, seldom bestow a thought upon Cricket; it is, nevertheless, esteemed and enjoyed by the people of other counties, especially those round the metropolis, as a sport paramount, and practised in so great a degree, as nearly to exclude all other manly field recreations of a similar nature.

ANON *The Boy's Own Book*, 1855

Coming out to bat

The Philosopede

'It vent mitout a vheel in front,
And hadn't none pehind,
Von vheel was in the mittel, dough,
And it vent ash sure ash ecks,
For he shtraddled on de axeltree,
Mit der vheel petween his lecks.'

Having mounted it, his rapid progress astonished the spectators
as much as it gratified himself. But, alas for the pride of
success!

'His feet both shlipped outsideward shoost
Vhen at his extra shpede,
He felled oopon der vheel ov coorse;
De vheel like blitzen flew;
And Schnitzerl he vos schnitz in vact,
For id shlished him grod (*straight*) in two.'

ANON   The Boy's Own Book, 1878

The Young Velocipedist

The 'iron steed' has, of late, become well known, and generally
popular. Everywhere this 'highly-metalled animal' asserts its
existence. In America, we are told, no less than 100 patents
have been taken out, and persons of both sexes, and of all
ages, may be seen exercising themselves in riding-schools
especially constructed for the practice of iron-horsemanship.
Brother Jonathan, in fact, has been said to live on his velocipede. In Paris we hear of perilous rides down flights of steps,
and along parapets of quays, races in the Bois de Boulogne,
and races of the Prince Imperial along the Rue de Rivoli. Here,
in England, every day adds to the ranks of the velocipedists.
Grave, and even portly, city gentlemen have been observed
propelling themselves to their places of business, while trim
government clerks have actually ventured to wheel their
velocipedes to the awful doors of Downing Street. There are
'velocipede Derbies' at the Crystal Palace and the Agricultural
Hall. In Wales, as in America and France, the postmen deliver
letters by the aid of the velocipede. The iron steed has been

The Young Velocipedist

used in Shanghai, has been seen careering along in Japan, and has been imported into Barbary. It has been even observed in the air, for a sensationalist in Boston has travelled along a rope upon a velocipede with grooved wheels twenty feet above the heads of an astonished audience. In the face of all this evidence, we cannot disregard this latest mode of locomotion. Time will try it, and decide, far better than we can, whether velocipedes are of the things which posterity will not willingly let die. In the meantime we have no hesitation in introducing the machine to our young readers as a new, and thoroughly healthy, means of recreation, involving plenty of muscular exercise, and giving every opportunity for the exhibition of skill and dexterity.

ANON   *The Boy's Own Book*, 1878

Rules for the velocipedist:
'Place your velocipede in
such a manner that the
right side pedal shall be
upwards'

Sport for June

If the young fisherman now wishes for a day's fishing he need only get into the *Era* steamer, at Hungerford, and run up the river to Twickenham; between which place and Teddington he will get good fishing after the 4th of this month. There, too, he will find perch, dace, chub, and barbel. In Twickenham meadows he may fish with good effect. Should he fish for perch he must use a minnow; if for pike, he must use a snail, dace, gudgeon, or roach. Roach will bite at the baits prepared for the chub or dace. Carp generally live in deep holes, and bite close to the bottom. Chub will rise at a natural or artificial

THE PET LAMB.

THE DONKEY.

fly. In angling for gudgeon the bottom should be previously stirred up. As to pricklebacks and minnows, they had better consult the 'Book of Sports,' published by Darton and Clark, where they will find all that they can desire respecting the art of angling.

PETER PARLEY   *Peter Parley's Annual*, 1844

Breaking the ice

Skating

If we may judge of the popularity of the different sports and amusements by the amount of danger which we see incurred in their pursuit, we should say that none stands so high in public favour as Skating. Let any one go to the Regent's Park, or to the Serpentine in Hyde Park, two or three days after a frost has set in, and he will there see ample proof of our assertion, by witnessing the drags of the Royal Humane Society at full work in extricating those rash and impatient youths who have been so foolish as to venture upon the ice before it is strong enough to bear them, contrary to the urgent admonitions of the officers of that very benevolent society, by whose indefatigable exertions thousands have been rescued from an untimely grave.

'UNCLE CHARLES'   *The Boy's Own Book of Sports
and Games*

eft, above:
ook at Laura and
alter with their pet
mb. It will eat from
alter's hand and has let
aura tie a blue ribbon
und its neck.'
elow: 'Well, Tom, you
ve a fine steed.'
om Happy Children's
ets

The Stanhope

The Stanhope skate, introduced by Mr Dean, the well-known bootmaker of the Strand, differs from all others in having but two wheels, and these wheels are arranged like the wheels of a bicycle, one large one in front and another smaller one under the heel. The front roller or wheel is firmly fixed in a metal frame to the metal sole or slipper of the skate. The hind wheel is acted upon by a strong spring, which is regulated by a screw to the weight of any skater, in order that, by changing the pressure of the body from the sole, to the heel, the spring may act as a retarding brake on the hind wheel, and enable the skater to check himself when in full career. The mechanism is the simplest known, and cannot fail to be popular, though it takes a much longer time to master the initiatory difficulties by the beginner than it does by the use of the Plimpton skates. The Stanhope skates, like the Spiller and other skates, may be bought for private use. This is not the case with the Plimpton skates, which are only sold to those who have obtained licence or concession for their use.

EDMUND ROUTLEDGE (Ed.)   Every Boy's Book, 1876

Alleys and Taws

In ancient times, when we were boys, and indulged in the luxury of marbles, they were very different from their present form. They were made of stone, nicely polished, and some of them, called 'alleys,' of the purest marble. Many of the stone marbles were beautifully variegated, and now and then a fancy pet was treasured under the name of 'taw,' which had somewhat the virtues of a talisman, for to 'lose it or to give it' were 'such perdition,' as Othello says, as could never be exceeded. Of late years, marbles, like all other matters, have undergone considerable change. Foreign marbles have been introduced, prodigiously cheaper, it is true, than our old English marbles, but infinitely worse; and various kinds of 'patent marbles' have had their day. Some of these go by the name of Dutchmen, others are called Frenchmen, and others again Chinamen, while it is not quite impossible to procure some right old English marbles, which, if they can be procured, are still the best. We would advise all marble players to procure these, if they

can, as 'marbles' is a royal game, and ought to be duly honoured.

How to Shoot your Marble.   The art of holding a marble to shoot it properly seems to be lost among our London boys, who are generally content to throw one marble at another, or if they shoot it to hold it in the turn of the fore-finger, forcing it out by the thumb, which is placed behind it. This, in our boyish days, was held to be a very illigitimate way of proceeding, derogatory to the true marble-player, and bore the dishonourable appellation of 'fulking,' and any one who made it his rule to hold a marble in such a manner was looked upon as a charlatan, or almost a cheat. The true way to hold your taw is to place it between the point of the fore-finger and the first joint of the thumb, and to propel it from the nail of the thumb with strong muscular force; and so great was the skill attained by many boys, that they would sometimes strike a marble at five yards' distance, and frequently shoot one to six or seven.

EDMUND ROUTLEDGE (Ed.)   *Every Boy's Book*, 1876

The Humming Top

These cannot easily be made, but can very easily be purchased by those who are so lucky as to have the money. They are made hollow, having at their crown a peg, round which is wound a string; this, being pulled through a kind of fork, gives motion to the top, and sets it spinning – the fork and the string being left in the spinner's hand. In spinning the top, care should be taken to wind the string firmly and evenly on the peg; and when it is pulled out, neither too much nor too little force should be used, and a firm and steady hand should be employed, while the top should be held in a perpendicular position. The string should be drawn with a steadily increasing force, or the top will not hum properly.

PEG-TOP

There are various kinds of Peg-tops, and they also vary in shape, some being much rounder than others. Those are the best which are shaped like a pear. There is also great variety as regards the shape and size of the peg, which in some tops is short and thick, in others long and tapering. Again, tops are made of different kinds of wood, some being made of deal, others of elm, some of yew-tree, and others of box-wood. These last are the Boxers so highly prized. Some of the very best tops are made of lignum vitæ, with long handsome pegs.

SPANISH PEG-TOP

The Spanish peg-top is made of mahogany. It is shaped some what like a pear; instead of a sharp iron peg, it has a small rounded knob at the end. As it spins for a much longer time than the English peg-top, and does not require to be thrown with any degree of force in order to set it up, it is extremely well adapted for playing on flooring or pavement.

    EDMUND ROUTLEDGE (Ed.) *Every Boy's Book*, 1876

Playing for Money

Harry put his hand into his pocket, and brought forth three pennies. 'I thought I had more money,' he said, 'let me see: I paid two-pence for having my box of dominoes mended, a penny for my hoop-stock, – then the lollypops, crackers, and the odd penny I gave Mother Griffin, at the toy-shop, to take back my black-handled knife that she gave me a bargain, because it was hurt in the hinge. Altogether, with the two-pence I lost to Willy Soames at Beggar my Neighbour – it is right, I dare say.'
'You dare say!' said Edward, smiling; 'and is that the manner in which you keep your accounts, Harry? Besides,' he added, gravely, 'I did not know that you played cards for money.'
'Oh, no! not for money exactly, – only a farthing a game, which is nothing, you know – just enough, as papa says, when he plays long whist, six-penny points – (which I shall play when I am a man) – just enough to create excitement.'
'Create excitement!' repeated Edward Millar, who, fortunately, had been taught to reflect upon both words and acts; 'that is the very thing we ought to avoid; because, when we are excited, neither our judgment nor our temper can have fair play.'

Tricks with cards

'Then that is the reason, I suppose, why papa looks so stupid,
and yet gets so cross, whenever he loses – if it be only a sixpence, which is nothing to him, for he gives away scores and
scores of shillings.'

MRS S. C. HALL   The Juvenile Budget, 1840

One in the Hand

A sieve, a string, a stick, and a lump of bread, or a pocketful
of corn, were all the arms and ammunition we required; for
our object was to capture them alive, carry them home, and
feed them until the Spring came, when they were again restored
to liberty. A little shed, the corner of a wall, or the stem of a
large old tree, were the sheltering places we selected; when
having reared up the sieve, so as to rest on the edge of the
stick, and scattered a few crumbs, or a little corn, upon the
snow, we retreated to reconnoitre from our hiding-place,
keeping hold of the end of the string, and peeping out, you
may be sure, about every minute or so; when, waiting a favourable moment, until sometimes as many as half-a-dozen birds
were seen pecking about the sieve, we gave the string a pull,
and down it came. Oh! what a running there was then; and
very often in our eagerness to seize the birds which were under
the trap, one or two would escape. Although it was wrong to
deprive the birds of their freedom, still, somehow, we thought
that we were showing them the greatest of kindness, by taking
them home, and feeding them well, when so little food was to
be found in the fields. Bless you! we never once thought how
we should like being served so ourselves.

       THOMAS MILLER   *The Boy's Own Country Book*

Effects of Hydrogen on the Voice

Make a hole through a wine cork of sufficient size to admit a smaller cork; through which make another hole, and fix it into the larger one. Tie the corks thus fixed into the neck of a bullock's bladder, previously exhausted of air; let a tube from a bottle generating hydrogen pass very tightly through the aperture in the small cork, and the gas will distend and fill the bladder. The instant it is full, withdraw the inner cork, and either prevent the escape of the gas by means of the thumb, or cork it closely, till the operator is ready to *breathe the gas*; to do which, he should put the open cork into his mouth, and take *one* inspiration, when on immediately speaking, his voice will be remarkably shrill. The effect will pass off in a few seconds.

ANON *Parlour Magic*

Conjuring

To furnish the ingenious youth with the means of relieving the tediousness of a long winter's, or a wet summer's evening – to enable him to provide, for a party of juvenile friends, instructive as well as recreative entertainment, without having recourse to any of the vulgar modes of killing time – to qualify the hero of his little circle to divert and astonish his friends, and, at the same time, to improve himself, are the principal objects of the following little Work.
The boy whose wonder and curiosity have been excited by the

experiments of the scientific lecturer, the illusions of the ventriloquist, or the deceptions of the exhibitor of feats of manual dexterity, will here find many of these mysteries unveiled, and plain directions for performing them, divested, as far as possible, of scientific or technical language. Many of the descriptions are strictly original, and now, for the first time, appear in print; and especial care has been taken to introduce only such Experiments as are adapted for performance at the parlour or drawing-room table or fire-side, and such as are practicable without expensive chemical or mechanical apparatus, and require no implements beyond those which any ingenious youth may readily furnish from his own resources, or at a trifling expense.

Another object of these pages is to inform, without being dryly scientific, by imparting interesting facts, to stimulate the young experimentalist to inquire into the laws that regulate them, by aiding him to acquire dexterity of practice, to smooth the road to the development of principles, – and, above all, to enable him to excape an imputation which every boy of spirit would consider the depth of disgrace, that of being 'No Conjuror!'

ANON   *Parlour Magic*

Acoustic Rainbow

A sounding-plate, made of brass, nine inches long, and half a line in thickness, covered with a layer of water, may be employed to produce a rainbow in a chamber which admits the sun. On drawing a violin bow strongly across the plate, so as to produce the greatest possible intensity of tone, numerous drops of water fly perpendicularly and laterally upwards. The size of drops is smaller as the tone is higher. The inner and outer rainbows are very beautifully seen in these ascending and descending drops, when the artificial shower is held opposite to the sun. When the eyes are close to the falling drops, each eye sees its appropriate rainbow; and four rainbows are perceived at the same time, particularly if the floor of the room is of a dark colour.

ANON   *Parlour Magic*

To Exhibit The Magic Lantern

The lamp being lighted and the room darkened, place the machine on the table, at some distance from the white wall or suspended sheet, and introduce into the slit one of the sliders with the figures inverted. If the movable tube be then pushed in, or drawn out, till the proper focus be obtained, the figures on the slider will be reflected on the wall, in their distinct colours and proportions, with the appearance of life itself, and of any size, from six inches to seven feet, according to the distance of the lantern from the wall. Movements of the figures are easily made by painting the subject on two glasses, and passing the same through the groove.

ANON   *The Boy's Own Book*, 1855

What wonders may be brought to pass By the optician's magic glass

Camera Lucida

Opposite to the place or wall where the appearance is to be make a hole of at least a foot in diameter; or, if there be a high window with a casement of that dimension in it, this will do much better, without such hole or casement opened. At a convenient distance, to prevent its being perceived by the company in the room, place the object or picture intended to be represented, but in an inverted situation. If the picture be transparent, reflect the sun's rays by means of a looking-glass, so that they may pass through it toward the place of represen-

Camera Lucida

tation; and, to prevent any rays from passing aside it, let the picture be encompassed with some board or cloth. If the object be a statue, or a living creature, it must be enlightened by casting the sun's rays on it, either by reflection, refraction, or both. Between this object and the place of representation put a broad convex glass, ground to such a convexity as that it may represent the object distinctly in such place. The nearer this is situated to the object, the more will the image be magnified upon the wall, and the further, the less; such diversity depending on the difference of the spheres of the glasses. If the object cannot be conveniently inverted, there must be two large glasses of proper sheres, situated at suitable distances, easily found, by trial, to make the representation correct. This whole apparatus of object, glasses, etc., with the persons employed in the management of them, are to be placed without the window or hole, so that they may not be perceived by the spectators in the room, and the operation itself will be easily performed.

ANON   The Boy's Own Book, 1855

Blowing Bubbles

If my young friends were to make use of hydrogen gas, instead of their breath, to inflate their soap bubbles, they would then have real gas balloons. To do this is very easy. Get some iron-filings, put them into a common wine-bottle, pour on then half-a-pint of water, into which put about half an ounce of sulphuric acid; the gas will then come off in abundance during the effervescence that ensues, and may be easily collected in a bladder, having the small end of a tobacco pipe inserted at its orifice. Then dip the bowl into the soap-suds, and squeeze the bladder, and your bubbles will be filled with hydrogen gas, and will immediately rise high in the air, and if they can get out of doors they will rise out of sight. This will be a more amusing sight than your common soap bubbles, which do not rise so high; and, some people would say, a vast deal more Philosophical.

PETER PARLEY   Peter Parley's Annual, 1854

The Bullock's Eye

Procure a fresh bullock's eye from the butcher, and carefully thin the outer coat of it behind; take care not to cut it, for if this should be done the vitreous humour will escape, and the experiment cannot be performed. Having so prepared the eye, if the pupil of it be directed to any bright objects, they will appear distinctly delineated on the back part precisely as objects appear in the instrument we are about to describe. The effect will be heightened if the eye is viewed in a dark room with a small hole in the shutter, but in every case the appearance will be very striking.

EDMUND ROUTLEDGE (Ed.) *Every Boy's Book*, 1876

How to Make an Air-balloon

The best shape for an air-balloon, or rather a gas-balloon, is that of a pegtop. And in preparing the gores proceed as follows: Get some close texture silk, and cut it into a form resembling a narrow pear with a very thin stalk. Fourteen of these pieces will be found to be the best number; and, of course, the breadths of each piece must be measured accordingly. When sewing them together, it will be of advantage to coat the parts that overlap with a layer of varnish, as this will save much trouble afterwards, and hold the silk firmer in its place during the stitching. The threads must be placed very regularly, or the balloon will be drawn out of shape, and it will be found useful if the gores are covered with a interior coating of varnish before they are finally sewn together. Take care not to have the varnish too thick. To the upper part of the balloon there should be a valve opening inwards, to which a string should be fastened, passing through a hole made in a small piece of wood fixed in the lower part of the balloon, so that the aeronaut may open the valve when he wishes to descend; and this should be imitated on a small scale, so that the young aeronaut may be perfectly familiar with the construction of a balloon. The gores are to be covered with a varnish of India-rubber dissolved in a mixture of turpentine and naphtha. Over the whole of the upper part should be a net-work, which should come down to the middle with various cords, proceeding from it to the circumference of a circle about two feet below the balloon.

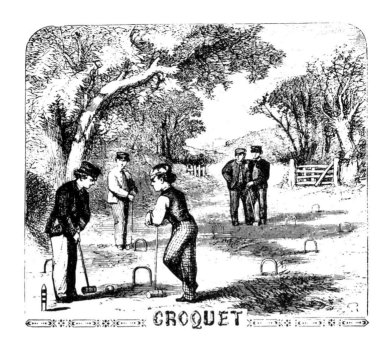

CROQUET

The circle may be made of wood, or of several pieces of slender cane bound together. The meshes should be small at top, against which part of the balloon the inflammable air exerts the greatest force, and increase in size as they recede from the top.

The car is made of wicker-work; it is usually covered with leather, and is well varnished or painted. It is suspended by ropes proceeding from the net which goes over the balloon. Balloons of this kind cannot be made smaller than six feet in diameter, of oiled silk, as the weight of the material is too great for the air to buoy it up. They may be made smaller of thin slips of bladder, or other membrane glued together, or of thin gutta-percha cloth, which is now extensively used for this purpose; with this they may be made a foot in diameter, and will rise beautifully.

How to fill a balloon

Procure a large stone bottle which will hold a gallon of water, into this put a pound of iron filings, or granulated zinc, with two quarts of water, and add to this by degrees one pint of sulphuric acid. Then take a tube, either of glass or metal, and introduce one end of it through a cork, which place in the bottle, then put the other end into the neck of the balloon, and the gas will rise into the body of it. When quite full withdraw the tube, and tie the neck of the balloon with strong cord very tightly. If freed it will now rise in the air.

EDMUND ROUTLEDGE (Ed.) *Every Boy's Book*, 1876

Timbromania

Our young readers may vainly turn over the pages of any existing dictionary to find the scientific alias of the heading of this article. We trust the omission will be soon supplied, *Philately*, or Postage Stamp Collecting, having reached the dignity of a recognised science.

The word is the English rendering of the French term *Philatelie*, bestowed by a distinguished Parisian amateur in substitution for what was called *timbromania*, the latter portion of which word caused an unpleasant association of ideas, and gave rise to many a sneer from the wiseacres who had not sense enough to understand the real utility of the pastime. . . .

To schoolboys in general be ascribed the honour of introducing the elegant and instructive fancy forming the subject of our dissertation. The young students of the college of Louvain in particular claim to have been the earliest collectors: thence the fancy spread over France and Germany, inoculating many an English pupil in continental seminaries, by whom it was transmitted home. Some Louvain scholars informed us last year that it had been long prohibited by the professors, as tending to induce inattention to their regular tasks! We think this a mistaken notion; convinced that a knowledge of geography, history, and the values of foreign coins is materially facilitated by the study of postage stamps; which, moreover, induces neatness, regularity, and a sure refuge from ennui on a rainy day.

EDMUND ROUTLEDGE (Ed.) *Every Boy's Book*, 1876

The Pretty Automata

ANN: I don't think I know very well what automaton means, aunt Susan; but I want to see one very much, because I have heard my cousins tell how very pretty they were.

AUNT: An automaton is an image, which, after being wound up, goes by the machinery within it, without any other help.

ANN: Are steamboats and windmills automata?

AUNT: No, my dear, because they are moved by wind and by steam; and the moment the wind, or the steam, is taken away, they stop. A clock is an automaton, because it moves entirely by its own machinery. Mr Maelzel's images are constructed upon similar principles: and all their wonderful feats are the result of his own knowledge of mechanical powers.

ANN: Do tell me about them.

AUNT: First, there was the Chess-player, an image dressed like a Turk; who sat at the board, and played as good a game of chess as if he had brains in his wooden skull. He shook his head, and rapped the board with his fingers, when his adversary made a move contrary to the rules of the game; and when he had the king in his power, he called 'Echec!' which is the French word for 'Check!'

Then there was a large Trumpeter, dressed in scarlet uniform, whose music was enough to make one's heart leap. The children were particularly delighted with the little figures in the carousel.

ANN: What is the meaning of *carousel*?

AUNT: It is the name of a military game in France. The scenery represents a circus with a fountain in the centre; and a number of little figures ride round the circus, performing feats to excite the wonder of the spectators.

One, called the Spanish Lancer, catches a little cap on the point of his lance, without stopping his horse, and rides off with it in triumph. Here is a print of him.

ANN: He looks like a real boy; but I think the horse looks clumsy.

AUNT: That is because he is a wooden horse, with jointed legs. You cannot expect him to canter quite as well as a real horse. Here is another of the figures, called the Marksman of Madrid. With a pistol not bigger than your thumb, he aimed at a little bird on a post. The pistol went off with real fire and smoke, and the bird fell down dead.

Another was a famous Vaulter. He jumped over standards, placed at a height which might be called *immense*, when com-

Pleasing and health-giving feats

pared with him and his horse; yet he was always sure to alight safely on his saddle.

A slow awkward Clown was pursued by a hungry Horse, who at last overtook him and snatched his cap from his head.

His friend Harlequin came to his rescue; but Harlequin's horse behaved very ill. He kicked, and plunged, and reared, and finally threw his poor rider off entirely. This made the little children laugh greatly.

The little girl who danced the Wreath-dance on horseback was as graceful as any of them. I cannot tell you half the feats these automata performed. If ever Mr Maelzel comes to London again, I will send for you, and take you to see them.

MRS CHILD The Girl's Own Book, 1848

Intery Mintery

A company of children all place the fore-fingers of their right hands, side by side, upon the knee of the one who is to begin the game. This one touches each one by turns, saying, 'Intery, Mintery, Cutery-corn, Apple-seed, and Apple-thorn; Wire, Brier, Limber-lock; five geese in a flock; sit and sing, by a spring, o-u-t and in again.' The one whose finger she happens to touch when she says, 'In again,' must pay any forfeit the others please to appoint. Sometimes she runs away, and the others have hard work to catch her.

MRS CHILD The Girl's Own Book, 1848

Lady Queen Anne

We will imagine five little girls engaged in this play, and their names may be Fanny, Lucy, Mary, Ellen and Jane.
A ball, or pincushion, or something of the kind, having been procured, Fanny leaves the room or hides her face in a corner, that she may not see what is going on, while her companions range themselves in a row, each concealing both hands under her frock, or apron. The ball has been given to Ellen, but all the others must likewise keep their hands under cover, as if they had it. When all is ready, Fanny is desired to come forward, and, advancing in front of the row, she addresses any one she pleases (for instance, Lucy) in the following words:

Lady Queen Anne she sits in the sun,
As fair as a lily, as brown as a bun,
She sends you three letters, and prays you'll read one.

LUCY: I cannot read one unless I read all.
FANNY: Then pray, Miss Lucy, deliver the ball.

Lucy, not being the one who has the ball, displays her empty hands; and Fanny, finding that she has guessed wrong, retires, and comes back again as soon as she is called. She then addresses Mary in the same words, 'Lady Queen Anne,' etc.; but she is still mistaken, as Mary has not the ball. Next time Fanny accosts Ellen, and finds that she is now right; Ellen producing the ball from under her apron. Ellen now goes out, and Fanny takes her place in the row. Sometimes the real holder of the ball happens to be the first person addressed.

MRS CHILD *The Girl's Own Book*, 1848

A game of draughts

Legerdemain

To Astonish a Large Party
With some lycopodium, powder the surface of a large or small
vessel of water; you may then challenge anyone to drop a piece
of money into the water, and that you will get it with the
hand without wetting your skin. The lycopodium adheres to
the hand, and prevents its contact with the water. A little
shake of the hand, after the feat is over, will dislodge the
powder.

How to Make Eggs Dance
Boil an egg hard, and break off a little piece of the shell at
either end; then thrust in a quill filled with quick-silver and
sealed at each end. As long as the egg is warm it will continue
to dance.

Luminous Writing
Place a small piece of solid phosphorus in a quill, and write
with it upon paper. If the writing be then taken to a dark room
it will appear beautifully luminous.

The Obedient Watch
Borrow a watch from a person in company, and request the
whole to stand around you. Hold the watch up to the ear of
the first in the circle, and command it to go; then demand his
testimony to the fact. Remove it to the ear of the next, and
enjoin it to stop; make the same request of that person, and
so on throughout the entire party. You must take care that
the watch is a good one. Conceal in your hand a piece of
loadstone, which so soon as you apply it to the watch, will
occasion a suspension of the movements, which a subsequent
shaking, and withdrawing of the magnet will restore. For the
sake of shifting the watch from one hand to the other, apply it
when in the right hand to the left ear of the person, and when
in the left hand to the right ear.

An Egg put Into a Phial
To accomplish this seeming incredible act, requires the following preparation: You must take an egg and soak it in strong
vinegar; and in process of time its shell will become quite soft,
so that it may be extended lengthways without breaking; then
insert it into the neck of a small bottle, and by pouring cold
water upon it, it will re-assume its former figure and hardness.
This is really a complete curiosity, and baffles those who are
not in the secret to find out how it is accomplished.

A well conducted party game, from *Home for the Holidays*

Hoar Frost Made to Order

Place a sprig of rosemary or any other garden herb in a
glass jar, so that when it is inverted, the stem may be down-
wards, and the sprig supported by the sides of the jar; then
put some benzoic acid upon a piece of hot iron, so that the
acid may be sublimed in the form of a thick white vapour.
Invert the jar over the iron, and leave the whole untouched
until the sprig be covered by the sublimed acid in the form of a
beautiful hoar frost.

ANON   *The Boy's Own Treasury*, 1860

Charades

The French have made themselves singularly famous by their
'*petits jeux*,' as they call them. Their inability to sit still for
more than half an hour has forced them to invent a long list
of amusing excuses for locomotion. They have their '*Pigeon
Vole*,' and '*Main Chaude*' or '*Berlingue*' and '*Chiquette*,' and
a thousand other receipts for making a long evening short.
But the most celebrated of all these *petits jeux*, are their
'*Charades en Action*.' *Pigeon Vole*, and all the rest, have given
way to these Acting Charades. No birth-day is allowed to
pass without playing at them. The young and the old both
delight in the game, and invariably choose it. The old people
lay aside their dignity with a look of jovial martyrdom, and

184

laugh more than any one else; whilst – as if to apologise for their apparently unbecoming levity – they tell you 'they do like to see young people enjoying themselves.'

Some persons have even acquired a kind of reputation as Charade actors, and are in such request that invitations shower down from all quarters; and if they can only be engaged, it is looked upon as a kind of certificate that the party is sure to be a good one.

Lately, the game has been introduced into the drawing-rooms of a few mirth-loving Englishmen. Its success has been tremen-

Two simple charades
OPPOSITE *Gardening*
RIGHT *Leg-horn*

dous. Cards have been discarded; and blind-man's buff, forfeits, and hunting the ring been utterly abandoned. On Christmas-day it has been looked forward to, and entered into with as much energy as the sainted plum-pudding itself. We have seen it played among literary circles with unbounded mirth. We have seen philosophers and poets either acting their parts with all the enthusiasm of school-boys, or puzzling their brains to find out how they could dress as Henry VIII, with only a great coat and a 'gibus.'

THE BROTHERS MAYHEW *Acting Charades*

Green Fire

Put into a glass tumbler two ounces of water, and add first a piece or two of phosphorus, about the size of a pea, then thirty or forty grains of chlorate of potass, then pour upon the mass, by means of a funnel with a long neck reaching to the bottom of the glass, five or six drachmas of sulphuric acid. As soon as the acid comes in contact with the ingredients, flashes of fire begin to dart from under the surface of the fluid, when this takes place, drop into the mixture a few pieces of phosphuret of lime: this will immediately illume the bottom of the vessel, and cause a stream of fire, of an emerald green colour, to pass through the fluid.

WILLIAM MARTIN *Indoor Sports*, 1858

The Little Gas-factor

Fill the bowl of the largest tobacco-pipe that can be procured with powdered coal (cannel coal answers best), and close the top of it by the application of pipe-clay, or, what is better, a mixture of sand and beer. When the covering is dry, place the bowl of the pipe in a clear fire; in a few minutes a dense smoke will issue from the stem, which on the application of lighted paper, will inflame, and will continue in a beautiful state of combustion as long as any gas continues to be distilled from the coal; and this gas will be sufficiently brilliant to illuminate the study of the little Gas-Factor.

ANON *The Boy's Own Book*, 1855

Amateur football

How bright is the morning, how fair is the day!
Come on, cousin Mary, come with me and play;
And yonder is Willie, I'll give him a call;
Do you take the mallets, I'll carry the ball.

But we'll make it a rule to be friendly and clever,
Even if we are beat, we'll be pleasant as ever;
'Tis foolish and wicked to quarrel in play,
So if I get angry, please send me away.

THE YOUNG VELOCIPEDIST

*A 'velocipede derby'
at the Crystal Palace*

Bead work

A great variety of beautiful work may be done with beads,
besides bags and purses. Necklaces strung in chains, or festoons,
or diamonds, or so as to form a hollow tube, furnish an amusing employment for little girls. They should be strung on
horse-hair, or a species of strong white grass, sold for that
purpose. Little shoulder-bracelets for infants' sleeves are easily
made, and are very pretty. Red, or blue, or white beads,
strung in diamonds, with a gold bead at every corner of the
diamond, are quite tasteful. Some form imitations of flowers,
by using beads of different shades and colours, after the same
fashion as flowers are marked on a sampler: in this case, the
beads must be sewed upon a narrow strip of linen, and all
the spaces between the flowers be filled with one colour, and the
linen afterwards lined with that narrow kind of ribbon called
taste. In all cases shoulder-bracelets should have an inch or
two of taste at each end, to tie them with; it should be of the
same colour as the beads.

MRS CHILD   *The Girl's Own Book*, 1848

The Young Card-Players

'Why, I thought you told me, as the only excuse for your card-playing, that it taught you to count; and now you are posed over a simple thing, which my dear little sister Phœbe, whose house I have just finished with those pretty bricks, could tell in a minute; yet she never plays cards –'

'No, you are all too religious for that,' sneered Harry.

'I am not ashamed of being thought too religious to do anything it is wrong to do,' replied Edward, gravely; 'but mamma says, she objects to cards on a moral, not a religious, principle. In the first place, to play them is to waste time – '

'You and your sister waste quite as much time upon music and drawing – though music you, Ned, cultivate only as an amusement – as I and Willy Soames and Tibby Jarvis expend upon cards.'

'Music, Harry, affords pleasure to others as well as to one's self. I often play, that my brothers and sisters may dance. My old grandfather, who is both lame and blind, delights in music; and my mother says, that music has a great tendency to soften and soothe the cares and anxieties of life, and I believe it; for if I take up my flute, when I am in bad spirits or out of humour, before I get half through an air or a rondo, my bad temper, as Phœbe says, has "all gone up the chimney."'

'Well, Edward, let it be as you will; but one must have some recreation, I suppose; and I am very glad that *my* mother does not keep me for ever hum-drumming – hum-drumming. Why all your amusements are studies!'

'Granted; and many of my studies are amusements.'

'Mamma,' retorted little Phœbe, who had joined the group, 'is one of the last persons in the world to keep us hum-drumm-

Ride to Bath.

189

ing; and I am sure, Harry, I can see over the hawthorn hedge into your garden, when you sit playing Beggar my Neighbour on the grass; and you young card-players look a great deal more hum-drum than we do, with our skipping-ropes, and our rocking-horses, and our merry hoops.'

'Yes, and you make a great deal of noise, my little lady Phœbe, and often put us out of our reckoning; and yet you do not consider such play to be waste of time!'

'Certainly not,' said Edward, who, though nearly fourteen, dearly loved a game at romps with his little brothers and sisters. 'Exercise is necessary for health's sake; and you would not have such a pain in your chest, Harry, if you flew a five-foot kite on the downs, or had a glorious game at cricket now and then, instead of sitting cramped up over a parcel of painted pasteboard.'

MRS S. C. HALL *The Juvenile Budget*, 1840

Games Lead to Vice

It is a general truth, that those persons who are good at games are good at nothing else. Generally speaking, good players are but miserable and useless persons. And when we consider how many other methods of exercise there are, quite as effectual, and far better; the fact that games have little or no tendency to improve the mind, but rather the reverse; the numerous methods of recreation to which resort may be had, which *do* elevate and improve the mind; the consequent waste of time in gaming, which might be spent in acquiring valuable knowledge; and the known positive tendency of games to immorality and vice – remains there a doubt, as to whether or not it were better to dismiss them?

THOMAS TEGG *A Present For an Apprentice*, 1848

SICKNESS & DEATH

In earlier children's stories, Death was the punishment for playing with fire or not eating your dinner. In mid-Victorian fiction, the dying child was no longer an Awful, but a Holy Example, specially called by God.

When the loss of a brother or sister was a common experience, the subject of death was an apt point of departure for moral lessons. A glorious ascent to heaven shielded the little reader from the realities and reassured him of his immortality. But the morbid and grisly descriptions of the physical aspects of death were calculated to terrorise him into submission and repentance.

In the face of other people's sickness and disablement, he was blackmailed into the unlikely emotions of gratitude and appreciation of his own happier lot. Health was a privilege, not a right, and you had to earn it by feeling sorry for people who hadn't got it.

Remorse and despair in bereavement were briskly dealt with in the solidarity of comforter and comforted and in the certainty of reunion. It was an age when you were taught to live for the temporal present, with a wary eye on the eternal future.

As the gulf between Nursery and Drawing-room widened with increasing middle-class prosperity, death became a grown-up concern behind closed doors. It was up to Cook, Nanny or the Governess to trot out the euphemisms when the physical nature of death became taboo.

The modern juvenile fare of sudden violent death sets out to entertain. The lingering and awful death presented to the little mid-Victorian reader was meant to be a terrible religious warning.

Old Solomon's Visitor

It was a bright morning in spring, and the cemetery on the out-skirts of the town looked more peaceful, if possible, than it usually did. The dew was still on the grass, for it was not yet nine o'clock. The violets and snowdrops on little children's graves were peeping above the soil, and speaking of resurrec-tion. The robins were singing their sweetest songs on the top of mossy grave-stones; happy in the stillness of the place. And the sunbeams were busy everywhere, sunning the flowers, lighting up the dewdrops, and making everything glad and pleasant. Some of them even found their way into the deep grave in which Solomon Whitaker, the old gravedigger, was working, and they made it a little less dismal, and not quite so dark.

Not that old Whitaker thought it either dismal or dark. He had been a gravedigger nearly all his life, so he looked upon grave-digging as his vocation, and thought it, on the whole more pleasant employment than most of his neighbours.

It was very quiet in the cemetery at all times, but especially in the early morning; and the old man was not a little startled by hearing a very small voice speaking to him from the top of the grave.

'What are you doing down there old man?' said the little voice. The gravedigger looked up quickly, and there, far above him, and peeping cautiously into the grave, was a child in a clean white pinafore, and with a quantity of dark brown hair hanging over her shoulders.

'Whoever in the world are you?' was his first question.

His voice sounded very awful, coming as it did from the deep of the grave, and the child ran away, and disappeared as suddenly as she had come.

Solomon looked up several times afterwards as he threw up fresh spadefuls of earth, but for sometime he saw no more of his little visitor. But she was not far away; she was hiding behind a high tombstone, and in a few minutes she took courage, and went again to the top of the grave. This time she did not speak, but stood with her finger in her mouth, looking shyly down upon him, as her long brown hair blew wildly about in the breeze.

Solomon thought he had never seen such a pretty little thing. He had had a little girl once, and though she had been dead more than thirty years, he had not quite forgotten her.

'What do they call you, my little dear?' said he, as gently as his husky old voice would let him say it.

'Dot,' said the child, nodding her head from the top of the grave. . . .

Old Solomon was digging a grave one day in a very quiet corner of the cemetery. Dot was with him, as usual, prattling away in her usual childish way.

'It's a tidy grave, is this,' remarked the old man, as he smoothed the sides with his spade; 'nice and dry, too; it'll do me credit.'

'It's a very nice one,' said Dot.

'Yes; it's like to be little when it's for a little girl; you wouldn't want a very big grave, Dot.'

'No,' said Dot; 'but you would want a good big one, wouldn't you, Mr Solemn?' The mention of his own grave always made Solomon go into one of his 'reverdies'. But he was recalled by Dot's asking quickly,

'Mr Solemn, is she a very little girl?'

'Yes,' said the old man; 'maybe about your size, Dot. Her Pa came about the grave. I was in the office when he called, and he said, 'I want a nice quiet little corner, for it is for my little girl!'

'Did he look sorry?' said Dot.

'Yes,' he said, 'folks mostly do look sorry when they come about graves.'

Dot had never watched the digging of a grave with so much interest as she did that of this little girl. She never left Solomon's side, not even to play with her doll. She was very quiet, too, as she stood with her large eyes wide open, watching all his movements. He wondered what had come over her, and he looked up several times rather anxiously as he threw up the spadefuls of earth. 'Mr Solemn,' she said, when he had finished, 'when will they put the little girl in?'

'Tomorrow morning,' said the old man, 'somewhere about eleven.'

Dot nodded her head, and made up her mind she would be in this corner of the cemetery at eleven o'clock. . . .

Dot ran up as soon as they were gone, and, taking hold of Solomon's hand, she peeped into the grave. The little coffin was at the bottom, and some of Dot's daisies were lying round it.

'Is the little girl inside there?' said Dot, in an awe-struck voice.

'Yes,' said Solomon, 'she's in there; poor thing; I'll have to fill it up now.'

'Isn't it very dark?' said Dot.

'Isn't what dark?'

'In there,' said Dot; 'isn't it very cold and dark for the poor little girl?'

'Oh, I don't know that,' said Solomon. 'I don't suppose folks feels cold when they are dead; anyhow, we must cover her up warm.'

But poor Dot's heart was very full; and sitting on the grass beside the little girl's grave, she began to cry and sob as if her heart would break.

'Don't cry, Dot,' said the old man; 'maybe the little girl knows nothing about it – maybe she's asleep like.'

But Dot's tears only flowed faster. For she felt sure if the little girl *were* asleep, and knew nothing about it, as old Solomon said, she would be waking up someday, and how dreadful it would be for her.

'Come, Dot,' said Solomon, at last, 'I must fill it up.'

Then Dot jumped up hastily. 'Please, Mr Solemn, wait one minute,' she cried, as she disappeared amongst the bushes.

'What ever is she up to now?' said the old gravedigger.

She soon came back with her pinafore full of daisies. She had been gathering them all the morning, and had hid them in a shady place under the trees. Then with a little sob, she threw them into the deep grave, and watched them fall onto the little coffin. After this she watched Solomon finish his work, and did not go home till the little girl's grave was made, as Solomon said, 'all right and comfortable.' . . .

'Mr Solemn,' she said, one day, 'shall you make *me* a little grave when I die?'

'Yes,' he said, 'I suppose I shall, little woman.'

Dot thought this over for a long time.

'I don't want to go into a grave,' she said; 'it doesn't look nice.'

'No,' said the gravedigger, 'you needn't be frightened; you won't have to go just yet. Why, you're ever such a little mite of a thing!'

'Please, Mr Solemn, when you die, who'll have to dig your grave, please?'

'I don't know,' said Solomon, uneasily; 'they'll have to get a new digger I suppose.'

'Maybe you'd better dig one ready when you've a bit of time, Mr Solemn.' . . .

Dot was taken suddenly worse, and even her mother knew that her little girl would not be long with her. She was very tender to Dot now; she would hold her little girl in her arms for hours together, for Dot was very weary, and liked to lie quite still, with her head on her mother's shoulder. And, at length, there came a long sorrowful day, when Dot's father stayed away from work, and Dot's mother sat all day beside the little bed, which they had brought down for the child to lie upon.

It was evening, and little Dot was sinking fast. She had hardly spoken all day, except to murmur her little prayer; but now old Solomon had come in, after his day's work, and was sitting beside her, holding her tiny hand in his.

She opened her eyes and smiled at him.

'Mr Solemn,' she asked, 'have you said it?'

'Said what, my dear?' replied the old man.

'My little prayer, Mr Solemn.'

'Yes, my dear; yes Dot; I've said it many a time, and, what's more, my dear, I'm an old sinner, but I do believe the Lord's heard me, and done it for me; I do believe He has.'

'I'm so glad,' said little Dot; and she smiled as she said it.

He stayed with her till it was quite late, and when he was coming away, she said, wearily:

'I'm so tired, Mr Solemn.'

'Are you, my dear,' said the old man.

'Please, Mr Solemn, say my little prayer for me tonight.'

Solomon knelt down by the side of the bed. Dot's father and mother knelt beside him, and little Dot clasped her hands and shut her eyes, whilst the old man prayed in trembling voice:

'Lord, dear Lord, wash us all tonight, and we shall be whiter

'Wash Me And I Shall Be Whiter Than Snow'

196

than snow. Wash me, and little Dot, and Dot's father and mother, for Jesus Christ's sake. Amen.'

Then he kissed Dot, and came away with a troubled heart.

The next morning, as he went to his work, he heard that his little girl was dead. 'What! my little darling,' said the old man, 'my little darling gone!' . . .

There was a little grave to be dug that day, and it was the hardest task Solomon ever had. The earth seemed to him as heavy as lead that morning; and many times he stopped and moaned, as if he could work no more. He sometimes looked up, as if he half expected to see his little Dot standing at the top of the grave. He almost thought he heard her merry laugh, and her dear little voice saying, 'Won't you say my little prayer, Mr Solemn?'

But this was his little Dot's grave, and she was dead. It could not be true; oh, it could not be true!

But, as the old man toiled on, a happier thought stole into his soul, and he thought he saw his little Dot, dressed in white, and walking with the angels, near the dear Lord, in the home above the blue sky. And it did old Solomon good to think of this. The grave was close to Lilian's; side by side they were to lie, for so her father had ordered it. For he loved little Dot for the care she had taken of his child's grave.

It was the day of the funeral – little Dot's funeral. Old Solomon was wandering among the trees of the cemetery, and every now and then stooping wearily to gather something from the ground. He was getting daisies to put in his little dear's grave.

They were very scarce now, and it gave him much trouble to collect them, and they looked very poor and frost-bitten when he put them together, but they were the best he could find, and, with trembling hands, he threw them into the grave.

It was a very quiet funeral. The gentleman and the lady and their two little girls came to it, and Dot's father and mother, and old Solomon did his sorrowful part.

And they looked down into the grave at the little white coffin lying amongst the daisies. Then all was over, and the robin sang his song on little Dot's grave.

Lilian's father ordered a stone exactly like that which he had put to his own child – a small white marble stone, and on the stone were these words –

'LITTLE DOT'

and underneath was Dot's text –

'Wash Me And I Shall Be Whiter Than Snow.'

Old Solomon toiled on, often lonely and sad. The neighbours said he was getting childish, for he often fancied his little Dot was alive, and he would look up from the graves and smile at her, as he used to when she stood at the top. And he often thought he heard her little voice whispering among the trees of the cemetery. And the words she whispered were always those of her little prayer. So Solomon grew to think of her as alive and not dead, and it comforted his old heart. 'For,' said he, 'it will not be very long before I shall see her again.'

Thus Solomon was troubled no longer at the thought of his own grave, or of who should dig it.

MRS WALTON Little Dot and Her Friends

The Little Child's Grave

Now, in a corner of the churchyard, under the stone wall, and by the side of a China rose, was a young child's grave. A little grave it was, lying by itself; yet there was a small path up to it; for the young child's mother oftentimes came thither in secret of an evening, when the place was still. Many daisies also grew upon it, for, albeit the mother knew it not, yet did many young angels consort thither, bringing live daisies, which they love, and causing them to blow in the same place many times over again. This little grave was beloved by the old grave under the yew, for he perceived how it was visited by angels; therefore he bade it speak to the other graves, that they might learn its excellence. So the little grave spoke and said – 'Behold, I am the last made of you all, and ignorant of many things! yet do the angels visit me, and oftentimes I hear the rustling of their wings about me. I am the resting place of young Christian innocence. My tenant, gathered like a virgin rose, felt not the blight of the world ere it died. Sweet was the last sigh of the little Christian on his mother's breast; pleasant his smile, as he sank smoothly away without a stain. Remember ye not his baptism at the holy font, and the sacred cross on his small forehead? How tenderly his mother bore him along to his second birth. She folded him close in her arms, close from the rude wind. The angels followed behind unseen. Now his young limbs are decayed; his bright blue eye has been eaten by worms; therefore do, mortals, blame me, who cover so sweet a thing; albeit, in truth, I am nothing else than the garner of its immortality; for the time shall come when the graves shall be opened, and then I also, who am but a little grave, will reveal my treasure . . . '

ANON *Morals From the Grave Yard*, 1838

Visiting little Emma

May Flowers; or Lucy Lynn

One evening I was strolling
Through a little country town:
The flowers were closing for the night,
And the sun was going down:
Musing, the old church-yard I sought,
Where the dead slept silently:
And I thought how sad a thing it was,
For the young and gay to die!
When, ah! a merry voice I heard,
And a bounding step brush by.

I turned, and saw a little child
Singing 'neath the hawthorn tree
That a green corner shaded: – there,
Happy child! – from sorrow free.
She pulled from its highest boughs
The beautiful May flowers,
Laughing the while they covered her,
With white and fragrant showers;
Aye! laughing as we only can
In childhood's earliest hours.

I said ''Tis late, my little girl,
To make a wreath tonight;
You should have twined it in the morn,
By the waking sun-beams' light.'
'I did make one, of cowslips, then;
And it decks the green today,
And it is much the prettiest there,
So do they, who've seen it, say.
But, then, it does not smell so sweet,
As a garland of white May.

And if you should be here again,
When the May-tree blooms, next year,
And come into the church-yard then,
You'll be sure to find me here;
Beneath the same old white May-tree,

May Flowers; or Lucy Lynn

Where the grass is always green,
And the sweet violets, at its root,
Are the bluest ever seen.
Then, don't forget to look for me;
And my name is Lucy Lynn.'

Ah! little knew that happy child,
As her heart with gladness leaped,
That her promise, made so gaily,
Strangely, sadly, would be kept.
Another checkered year passed by,
And another May-day came;
Within the church-yard's bounds I stood,
By the old tree white again; –
But I heard no sound of laughter,
No young voice call my name.

For, close beneath the Hawthorn,
There was a little grave,
And on its sides already,
The grass began to wave;
The simple words there written,
Were, 'Lucy Lynn, aged seven.'
And the falling hawthorn blossoms,
Above her still were driven;
But she scented not their sweetness,
For HER May-day was in Heaven.

ANON *Spring Flowers and Summer Blossoms for the Young and Good*

'Then with a little sob, she threw them into the deep grave
and watched them fall onto the little coffin.'
From *Little Dot and her Friends* (see page 195)

Squeeze Miss Peggy Down

. . . 'Let me see her,' said Charlie. 'Oh, she's dead. She's quite
dead. We'll bury her.'
'Well, so we will,' cried Susy.
So they each took a stick and began to dig a hole in grand-
mamma's garden. When they had dug a pretty large one, they
squeezed Miss Peggy down into it, and covered her with leaves.
'Now she's dead and buried,' said Charlie, 'let's go and think
about her. People always sit down and think about dead folks.'

ELIZABETH PRENTICE *Little Susy's Six Teachers*, 1879

The Suicide's Grave

'Alas! miserable grave that I am, set apart from the rest of the
graves! The nettles and nightshade crowd over me. The toads
make me their habitation. The slimy lizards crawl about me.
The grass grows on me rank and noisome. The dews refresh me
not; the angels visit me not. I am a solitary grave – the grave
of a suicide! All the other graves are holy; but I am not holy.
Over me was no prayer read as my tenant was committed to
the dust. The minister came not with his white robes and his
holy book. No crowd stood round with tears. I was dug in the
night, by the sexton, with his dusky lantern. The villagers
cross the churchyard on the other side for fear of me. I am
alone in the damp of the churchyard to my own thoughts, for
the other graves speak not with me.' Thus cried the melancholy
voice in the stillness of the night, and surprised the other graves.
Therefore they asked, who could tell the history of this sad
grave? To which the old grave made answer from under the
yew, and said, 'My friends, three days after the lightning struck
the tower was this grave made, the cause of which I have heard
from the sexton; for one night a stranger came with him into
the churchyard, and they two searched for this grave, and when
they found it, the sexton sate him down upon it, and told
concerning the suicide. You must know, then, that he who so
wickedly killed himself, and was here buried, was the son of
righteous parents, but took to evil ways in his youth. Evil
companions he had, whom he loved better than his father or
his mother. Oftentimes his mother spoke to him, calling him

back; but he would not listen. He forsook the church of his infancy. So his mother died of a broken heart, and he left his father in his old age, and crossed the seas to foreign countries, where he led a reckless life. Crimes untold were his. Ten times stained in guilt was his soul. At last God, who had borne with him a long time, left him to himself. What he did after this I do not know; but when many years had passed, and he came again to this village, so marked was his face with crime, that I remembered him not, albeit I had known him so well in the undutiful days of his youth. Much gold he brought with him when he came back to this village; but none would speak to him. So he went away again to some large city, where he lost all his money by gambling, and came back here and killed himself. Justly, then, is his grave without honour; for it is the grave of guilt ten times stained – guilt unwashed by the tears of repentance. Oh, thou suicide! if thou hadst but called back to remembrance thine early days, when thy mother led thee to the church, and gave thee a little prayer book! But now it is too late. There is no repentance in the grave!'

Thus spoke the old grave; and all the other graves said, 'Thou hast spoken well: the grave of guilt is without honour.'

ANON   *Morals from the Graveyard*, 1838

The Idiot Boy

One day the poor woman and her idiot boy were missed from the market-place, and the charity of some of the neighbours induced them to visit her hovel. They found her dead upon her very sorry straw bed, and the boy sitting beside her, holding her hand, weeping and singing her pitiful lay, while his body rocked to and fro. His song seemed more plaintive and touching than it had ever been before. He could not speak, but only utter a brute-like moan. Sometimes, however, he looked as if he comprehended what was said to him. On this occasion, when the neighbours spoke to him, he looked up with a tear in his eye, and, clasping the cold hand more tenderly, sung the strain of his mournful 'mam, mam,' in a softer and sadder key. The spectators, deeply affected, raised him from the body, and he surrendered his hold of the earthy hand without resistance, retiring in silence to an obscure quarter of the room. One of them, looking towards the others, said, 'Poor wretch! what shall we do for him?' At that moment he resumed his chant, and, lifting two handfuls of ashes from the hearth, on which he sat, sprinkled it on his head, and sung with a wild and heart-piercing pathos, 'Mam, mam, mamma!' In a few days the corpse of the poor woman was put into a shell, and taken away to the common burial-ground at the expense of the parish. It was carried in a chimney-sweeper's cart. There was mourning only of the sooty kind; there were no pall-bearers, mutes, undertakers, walking before, with other supernumeraries, nor were there any mourners behind; for the poor woman had no relatives or friends in the world. There was, however, the poor idiot clinging with his feeble hands to the back of the cart, every now and then laying his head on the coffin, which protruded behind, when the vehicle stopped, singing his mournful dirge, 'Mam, mam, mamma!'

He knew that his dead parent was in that box, for he had seen the two old parish women put her there and fill her up with sawdust. He knew not the meaning of the ceremony of sawdust and deal box, any more than he did that of the grave or the service read by the priest beside it, when he stood looking upon all that was going on, moaning inwardly, and chanting his fond requiem of sorrow. 'Stand out of the way!' said the gravedigger, as he pulled away the wooden log upon which the

Behold and bless the gentle flower That deck's the peasant's grave

coffin rested, while the bearers lifted it up by the ropes, prior to lowering it into the deep hole half full of water – the leaky part of the ground being used for parish paupers. 'Stand out of the way!' said the gravedigger, as he threw the log upon the heap of earth dug out of the grave, on which the idiot was standing, and which bruised his shoeless ankles.

The clergyman then read, 'Earth to earth, ashes to ashes.' The idiot started when he heard the thick clay soil fall on the coffin, and gave a howling kind of groan; his body rocked to and fro, and he muttered an incoherent gibberish, which interrupted the minister in his service. He was pushed rudely back; he tried to advance towards the pit-hole, when a strong arm laid hold of him and dragged him out of the churchyard, and took him to the workhouse . . .

PETER PARLEY   *Peter Parley's Annual*, 1868

The Hospital

Look at this picture well, you little, bright, happy children, who are well and strong, or even any afflicted like these, and be grateful for the cheerful homes, the loving friends, the comforts which surround you! Good generous people, pitying and loving little children, have sent enough money to support them, and have them taught trades to enable them to lead useful lives, though they are cripples.

See how busily at work this big girl is at the end of the form; but her crutches lying beside her tell only too plainly of her misfortune. Bad nursing in their babyhood, joyless unchildlike lives in crowded dirty streets, cause the children of the London poor to be wretched sufferers; and it is a piteous, touching sight to visit the hospitals which have been built for these poor little creatures. Everything is done for them that skill and kindness can do; but it is not like you at home in your beautiful nurseries, with your toys and books, your loving mother, and healthy little brothers and sisters making merry round. In each little bed is some poor, suffering child, tended by kind nurses certainly, but no mothers. Think of this, little ones, when inclined to be fractious and cross, and troublesome, and bless God who has made your lot so bright.

ANON   *The Children's Sunday Album*, 1881

Gentle Christians Pity Me

I'm a helpless cripple child,
Gentle Christians, pity me;
Once, in rosy health I smiled,
Blithe and gay as you can be,
And upon the village green,
First in every sport was seen.

Now, alas! I'm weak and low,
Cannot either work or play;
Tottering on my crutches, slow,
Thus I drag my weary way;
Now no longer dance and sing,
Gaily, in the merry ring.

Many sleepless nights I live,
Turning on my weary bed;
Softest pillows cannot give
Slumber to my aching head;
Constant anguish makes it fly,
From my heavy wakeful eye.

And, when morning beams return,
Still no comfort beams for me:
Still my limbs with fever burn,
Painful still my crippled knee,
And another tedious day
Passes slow and sad away.

From my chamber window high,
Lifted to my easy-chair,
I the village green can spy,
Once I used to frolic there,
March, or beat my new-bought drum;
Happy times! No more to come.

There I see my fellows gay,
Sporting on the daisied turf,
And, amidst their cheerful play,
Stopp'd by many a merry laugh;
But the sight I scarce can bear,
Leaning in my easy chair.

Let not then the scoffing eye,
Laugh, my twisted leg to see:
Gentle Christians, passing by,
Stop awhile, and pity me,
And for you I'll breathe a prayer,
Leaning in my easy chair.

ANON Original Poems, 1868

Flowers for Little Jane

One winter little Jane caught a cold, and was very ill. The doctor said he was afraid she would not be well for a long time, as she was a delicate child. So little Mary had to go to school by herself, but she missed her companion very much. And when the summer came still little Jane was ill, and could not leave her bed. Mary did not care to pluck the flowers on her way from school because Jane was not with her.
One day, when Mary was coming home, she saw a little boy gathering flowers. He said they were for a little sick sister at home, who was very fond of them.
All that evening Mary thought of what the little boy had told her, and then she thought of little Jane, and wondered if she would like to have some flowers too. So next day, after school, she gathered the prettiest flowers she could find, and brought

'Oh, you pretty flowers!
Thank you, dear Mary'

them to little Jane. When she saw them, Jane smiled and said, as she put out her hand, 'Oh you pretty flowers! Thank you dear Mary,' and she was so glad that the colour quite came into her cheeks. Jane's kind mother put the flowers into a glass of water on a little table by her bedside, and every day Mary brought fresh ones till Jane got well again.

Dear children, I hope you will be as kind to your little sick friends as Mary was to Jane.

ANON   *Children's Friend*, 1868

Mother's Last Words

A glimmering light was burning there,
Beside a woman on a bed:
A worn-out woman, ghastly pale,
Departing to the peaceful dead.

Two little boys in threadbare clothes,
Stood white and trembling by her side,
And listening to his mother's words,
The youngest of them sadly cried.

The elder boy shed not a tear,
Nor stirred a moment from his place,
But with a corner of the sheet,
He wiped his mother's cold damp face.

'And listen, John, before 'tis night,
My weary spirit will be free:
Then go, and tell the overseer,
For he must see to bury me.

Sickness and Death

You'll walk behind my coffin dears,
There's little more I have to crave,
But I should like to have my boys,
Just drop a tear beside my grave.

And then you'll have to leave this room,
Because the rent is not all paid,
Since I've been ill, I've let it run;
You know, I've barely earned your bread.

I don't owe much, I've minded that,
And paid it up, though hardly pressed,
So do not fret about my death
I know you'll not be left alone,
For God will send the Angel down,
To care for you, when I am gone.

I'm sure you will have daily bread,
For that the King gave strict command,
And all the wealth of London town,
Is in the power of his hand.

Good bye, - good bye, my children dear,
My happy soul is caught away:
I hear, I hear, my saviour call,
He calls me up, I cannot stay.' . . .

But sadly sobbed the little boys,
As from the bed of death they crept;
Upon the floor they sat them down,
And long and piteously they wept.

The dreary walls around them closed,
No father came to share their grief,
No friendly neighbour heard their cry,
None came with pity or relief.

They cried, until their tears were spent,
And darker still the chamber grew:
And then said little Christopher,
'Now Mother's dead, what shall we do?'

Mother's Last Words

So never join with wicked lads
To steal and swear, and drink, and lie,
For though you are but orphans here,
You'll have a Father in the sky.

I can't see plain, what you should do,
But God, I think, will make your way,
So don't go to the workhouse, dears,
But try for work, and always pray.'

The woman ceased, and closed her eyes,
And long she lay, as if at rest,
Then opened wide her feeble arms,
And clasped her children to her breast.

And then aloft her hands she raised,
And heavenward gazed with beaming eyes,
'I see, I see, the Angel comes,
I see him coming from the skies.

He stood behind them at the door,
And heard the growling Overseer,
Then touched his heart with sudden smart,
And brought an unexpected tear.

Then John rose up, and with his sleeve,
He wiped away the last sad tear,
'Well, we must go, as Mother said,
And tell the parish overseer.'

'But won't the Angel comes to us?'
'I cannot tell you,' John replied,
'I think he will,' said Christopher,
'My mother saw him, when she died.'

They stumbled up the broken stairs,
And pushed their way along the street,
Whilst out of sight, an Angel bright,
Walked close behind, with shining feet.

Sickness and Death

'Here, lads,' he cried, 'divide this bread,
You both look hungry, any way:
We'll see about the body, child,
And bury it on Wednesday.'

The hungry children ate the loaf,
And then the younger brother said
'Our mother told us right, you see,
That was all true about the bread.'

'It does seem so,' was John's reply,
'I say, Chris, shan't you be afraid
To go and sleep at home tonight,
All in the dark there with the dead?'

'Why should we, John? dead folks don't hurt,
She would not hurt us, if she could;
And as she laid upon the bed,
She looked so happy and so good.' . . .

When dimly dawned the light, they rose,
And Chris looked round with chattering teeth;
The sheet was spread from head to foot,
He knew his mother lay beneath. . . .

On Wednesday the people came,
And took the woman's corpse away;
Two little mourners walked behind,
And saw the grave wherein it lay.

Fast fell the tears upon their cheeks,
When little Christy raised his eyes,
And said, 'Oh, mother! How I wisn
I was with you above the skies.'

'Twas but the thought passed through his mind,
When a soft whisper seemed to come –
'Be patient little Christopher,
You are not very far from home.' . . .

Mother's Last Words

'We won't go to the workhouse, Chris,
But act like men, and do our best;
Our mother said, 'A crust well earned,
Was sweeter than a pauper's feast.'

'Oh yes, we'll work like honest boys,
And if our mother should look down,
She'd like to see us with a broom,
And with a crossing of our own.' . . .

'Twas one sultry summer's night,
When heavy lay the stifling air,
As John was dropping off to sleep,
He heard a softly whispered prayer,
He knew 'twas Chris, and did not stir,
And then he heard a gentle sigh;
It was the dear boy's happy soul,
Escaping to its home on high.

He left behind his wasted form,
He rose above the toiling folk,
Above the cross upon St Paul's
Above the fog, above the smoke.

And higher, higher, up he went,
Until he reached the golden gate,
Where night and day, in shining bands,
The holy angels watch and wait.

And he went in, and saw the King,
The Saviour, who for him had died,
And found once more his mother dear;
And little Chris was satisfied.

And there they both together wait,
Till John shall reach that happy home,
And often from the golden gate,
They watch in hope to see him come.

MRS SEWELL *Mother's Last Words*

Don't You Cry for Me, Kitty

The doctor shook his head slowly, as he sat on the three-legged stool.

'Do you want very much to be about again, my little man?'

'I'd like it,' said Jamie. 'Won't I soon be better?'

'You are very ill, my poor child. The pain in your leg is caused by an abscess which has formed there. I will send you some medicine to make you feel quieter and less restless. And Miss Howard – she is my niece – will see that you have all you want in the way of food. But we cannot do much for you, poor Jamie.'

There was a perplexed, bewildered look on Jamie's face. He stretched out one hand towards, Kitty, with a frightened, beseeching expression.

'Oh, Kitty! what does he mean? Must I never be well?'

'Jamie,' said the kind doctor, bending forward, and leaning with both hands on his stick, 'would you be afraid if I told you you could never be well?'

'I don't know,' Jamie said tremulously. 'Shall I always have pain? – always be thirsty?'

'Not if you love and trust in the Lord Jesus Christ, little Jamie. Not if you hunger and thirst after righteousness.'

'Did the lady tell you that, please?' Kitty could not help inquiring.

'Yes; Miss Howard told me of a little boy and girl who were hungering and thirsting up in these garrets. Jamie, you will not have to lie here much longer in pain and thirst. Will you be afraid to die, when you know that the Lord Jesus died that you might go to heaven?'

A little shudder passed over Jamie.

'Must I go now?' he asked, while a low sob was audible from Mrs Swindon, caused by memories of her youthful days, called up by the doctor's words.

'Not for a little while. I think you may yet live some weeks, perhaps even longer. But you will never be strong and well again I am afraid, little Jamie.'

Jamie's eyes roved about distressfully. 'I wish the lady was here,' he murmured. 'It frightens me.'

'If she were here, I think she would only tell you about the loving Lord Jesus Christ, and say that you must pray to Him. Shall I ask Him now to teach you about Himself, before I go?'

Kitty scarcely understood the proposal, but Jamie's look was one of eager assent, and the doctor knelt down upon the dusty,

A VISIT TO THE GRAVE.

unswept floor, beside the heap of straw. Mrs Swindon leaned against the wall, hiding her face. Kitty sank timidly on her knees. The doctor's prayer was very short and simple. Jamie and Kitty could understand every word.

'O God, we beseech Thee to look down upon poor little Jamie, in his pain and weakness, and to make him Thine own child. We beseech Thee to forgive him all his sins, and to give him a new heart, and to make him love Thee. Thou seest, O Lord, all who truly hunger and thirst after righteousness, and Thou hast promised that they shall be filled. We pray that all who are present may be led to know and love Thee. And we ask all this in the name and through the death of our Lord Jesus Christ. Amen.'

There was a moment's pause, and then the doctor rose from his knees, and Kitty rose, and Mrs Swindon went out of the

From Faithful Words, *a story with a moral: 'I am an old man and you are very young, but it may be you will die before me'*

room, sobbing too much to stay any longer. Jamie lay quite still and peaceful – no longer anxious and frightened. The doctor did not say much more, and he was obliged to go, as he had many other visits to pay that afternoon. When the children were again alone, Kitty crept up to Jamie's side.

'Oh, Jamie!' she began, and then the tears rose to her eyes, and she could hardly speak. But Jamie looked still quite calm.

'Don't you cry for me, Kitty. I won't be so frightened now. Maybe I shall be glad in a little bit. Sure the lady said we'd be answered if we prayed.'

Was not the promise already being fufilled, that all who 'hunger and thirst after righteousness' shall be filled?

ANON   Hungering and Thirsting

Fast to Corruption

When they came to the door, they perceived a kind of disagreeable smell, such as they never had smelt before: this was the smell of the corpse, which having been dead now nearly two days, had begun to corrupt: and as the children went higher up the stairs, they perceived this smell more disagreeably.

The body of the old man was laid out on the bed . . . The face of the corpse was quite yellow, there was no colour in the lips, the nose looked sharp and long, and the eyes were closed, and sunk under the brow; the limbs of the corpse, stretched out upon the bed and covered with a sheet, looked longer than is natural: and the whole appearance of the body was more ghastly and horrible than the children had expected . . . At last Mrs Fairchild said, 'My dear children, you now see what death is; this poor body is going fast to corruption. The soul I trust is in God; but such is the taint and corruption of the flesh, by reason of sin, that it must pass through the grave and crumble to dust . . .'

MRS SHERWOOD *The Fairchild Family*, 1869

The Dying Child

The sable shades of night closed in upon the earth, and the sky was dark and starless; and the lamp burnt dimly and faintly in a chamber where a little child was dying. His clasped hands rested on his bosom, and his little lips moved in still prayer. The long night passed away, and the golden beams of morning burst in at the casement and rested on the pillow of the dying child; and when he beheld the sudden burst of light, he thought in the pureness of his heart, that the gates of Heaven were wide open to receive him, and he said, 'Now, dearest mother, I may go, for heaven's holy gates are open for me!' And so his spirit passed like a dove freed from its prison-house, and amid that pure morning he went away, away, beyond the bright sun; to that happy country whose gates are not shut at all by day, and where there is no night.

MRS JERRAM *The Child's Own Story Book*, 1840

The Dead Baby

It was a very solemn day
When little baby died,
And dear papa and dear mamma
Were very sad, and cried.

She was so young – this wicked world
Her feet had never trod;
And yet her gentle soul was called
To go and live with God.

Pale was she as the rosebud white
Within her tiny hand;
Cold as the snow, that never falls
Upon the better land.

And she was in that lovely land,
The white-winged angel's home,
Where all the little lambs of Christ
One day shall surely come.

And very well her parents knew
That she was safely there,
But yet they felt 'twas hard to part
With that sweet infant fair.

And as they sat, and sadly wept,
Within the darkened room,
A little child came like a beam
Of sunshine in the gloom.

She quickly climbed their knees, and said
'Oh, no! you must not cry:
For little baby's gone to live
With Jesus, in the sky.'

And smiles upon their faces came,
Tho' still in grief they bowed,
Just as you've noticed, in a storm,
A rainbow in the cloud.

JOSEPHINE *Jottings for Juveniles*, 1862

Above: Tales of the Months and Seasons of the Year
Below: Shuttlecocks and hoops in the meadow
Both from *The Pleasant Verse and Prose Story Book*

Poor Little   Body

How easy it would be to hurt your poor little body! If it were to fall into the fire, it would be burned up. If hot water were to fall upon it, it would be scalded. If it were to fall into deep water, and not be taken out very soon, it would be drowned. If a great knife were run through your body, the blood would come out. If a great box were to fall on your head, your head would be crushed. If you were to fall out of the window, your neck would be broken. If you were not to eat some food for a few days, your little body would be very sick, your breath would stop, and you would grow cold, and you would soon be dead.

You see that you have a very weak little body.

Can you keep your own body from being sick, and from being hurt? You should try not to hurt yourself, but God only can keep your body from all harm, from fire, from water, from wounds and bruises, and all kinds of sickness. Kneel down and say to God, 'Pray, keep my poor little body from getting hurt.' God will hear you and go on taking care of you.

ANON   *The Peep of Day*, 1860

Anno Mundi

. . . 'Ten minutes after one,' she half said, half thought; 'in twelve more hours my baby will be a year old. She will have been one year in this world, one whole year, my precious baby – one whole year shall I have had my baby. How much she has known, how much she has learned in this one year! As we used to say at school, jestingly, *Anno Mundi! Year of the world One* for my baby, ere this tomorrow.'

Then, taking up her work, Sophia's mother, as she plied her needle, allowed herself to think of the coming years for her child. They were all years of the world; and prosperous, she hoped. The child promised a rare beauty, and health and temper; and, the mother added thereto, 'a wisdom' that she trusted would guide her in girlhood, youth, and age. But there she stopped; the mother hoped herself to go, before one sorrow touched the child – and yet, foolish mother, all her hopes were centered on the *Anno Mundi*.

But suddenly a start of the child aroused her; a slight cry, and

LITTLE EDWARD AND HIS FRIEND.

once again the arm was thrown unnaturally, and that so
decidedly, that the mother, too, sprang up. It was not the heat
of the weather that flushed the baby's cheek; it was not the
quiver of joy that trembled in the limbs. Ah! no, it was illness,
and illness of a kind that was strange to the mother. But the
mother knew it was fatal, and before the clock struck two, a
doctor had been summoned, and the baby's father, and all
around were busily engaged, trying to procure relief.

The attack was convulsions, produced by teething, and the
fever was very high.

It was just as the cottage clock struck one that the little one
gave a start, a sigh, and never moved again. Her one year of
life was perfected on earth, the year her mother, so short a
time before, had jestingly called 'the Anno Mundi'; that was
over and in its stead – oh, blessed child! – had commenced for
her 'the Anno Domini', or 'the Year of the Lord' – that year

This little pet is very very ill

which has no beginning nor ending; the same yesterday, today and for ever. The wisdom of this world was changed for heavenly wisdom, and the mother herself, in time, learnt to rejoice that that wisdom was her baby's.

SOPHIA KELLY The Little Lady

Willie Among the Angels

'Suffer little children to come unto me, and forbid them not.'
Ah! poor old Nurse Whitfield, she tries with these words to console herself for the loss of the little boy she had nursed from his birth, and whom she loved like her own.
He had always been very delicate, several of his sisters had

died, and the poor mother, who was obliged to live in London, was told that if she wanted to save this only boy, she must let him be brought up in the country.

So she let dear good Nurse Whitfield, who was with him when he was born, take him home with her, and he began to grow and thrive, and got on nicely till he was nearly four years old, and then he suddenly began to fail, and soon he took to his bed. His mother was sent for, and little Willie was numbered among the angels.

Just before he died he rose up in his bed and said, 'Oh, my Badgie!' – that was his little sister whom he could remember. So poor Nurse would often sit, years after, just as you see her here, looking at the toys he used to play with, and thinking that he and his little sister had been gathered in the Heavenly Shepherd's arms, and she ought not to 'forbid' it or complain, but only wait till her summons comes to rejoin them.

ANON   *The Children's Sunday Album*

Home to Heaven

So the next day her mamma said to her: 'Now my dear little Susy, I want you to spare mamma a little while. I want to go and see Mrs Wilson, whose baby is very ill. You can have dolly get into bed with you. I won't be gone long.'

On hearing this Susy began to cry.

'Susy, dear, if you were very ill, and going to die, don't you think Mrs Wilson would come and see me?'

'Would it comfort you if she came?'

'Yes, it would. And I want to go and comfort her, because perhaps very soon she won't have any little baby.'

'Let mamma go, Susy, like a good girl,' said Mrs Love. 'I'll stay with you while she's gone.'

'Yes,' said Mr Ought, 'Let her go.'

'Do go, dear mamma,' said Susy. 'I know you won't be gone long from your own child!'

Her mamma smiled, and Mr Ought said to her: 'Susy, you and I are getting to be very good friends. One of these days, if you

have a little Susy of your own, I will be her friend too, and help
her to be a comfort to you.'
Susy smiled, and began to think so much about having a little
Susy of her own, that she was surprised when her mamma came
back, to see her so soon.
'Did you see the little baby, mamma?'
'Yes, I saw it. It is very ill. It is going to die.'
'When it is dead will they bury it in the ground?'
'Yes, darling.'
'Then will they go home and leave it all alone?'
'Susy, I once read a very sweet sentence about that. I will
repeat it to you. "It is not that we go home, and leave our
friends behind; no, it is they that are gone to the better home,
and have left us behind." That dear baby will get home before
its dear mamma.'
'Home to heaven,' said the angel Faith, drawing nigh.
'I should think it would be very glad when it got there,' said
Susy. 'I suppose it would be looking round to see if Mr Pain
had got to heaven too. And when he found it hadn't it would be
very glad.'

ELIZABETH PRENTISS   *Little Susy's Six Teachers*, 1879

Dear Mother, Let me Go!

'Mother, dear mother, do not seek
To keep me from my Saviour's breast;
Oh, dry those sad tears from thy cheek,
Thy darling soon will be at rest.

Oh, would you keep me, mother dear,
From Him who ever loved me so?
I do not wish to linger here;
Mother, dear mother, let me go!

Dear Mother, Let me Go!

I seem to hear my Saviour's voice,
I seem to see his gentle smile;
Oh, mother, can you not rejoice?
We'll part but for a little while.

'For sinners such as she I died,'
I seem to hear him say to thee;
'Keep not my ransomed from my side,
But let thy darling come to Me.'

With praise to Him who died for me,
Mother your heart should overflow;
Then do not seek to hinder me,
Mother, dear mother, let me go!'

'Yes,' cried the mother, 'Go, my child;
The Saviour calls – He loves you best;'
Mary looked up and sweetly smiled,
Then closed her eyes – and was at rest.

ANON   *The Sunday School Magazine*, 1853

And often after sunset, Sir,
When it is light and fair,
I take my little porringer
And eat my supper there
      From Wordsworth's
      Poems for the Young

Father's Accident

'Tramp, tramp, footsteps came nearer; they stopped at the gate, and I saw – children, it makes me shiver now to tell it – your father brought home lying on a door!

'I didn't scream nor speak when the men he had been working with brought him in and rested him on the long dresser. Patrick Morrough, a good natured Irishman, came up to me, and said something about my cheering up, he wasn't quite dead . . .'

'He wasn't quite dead'

J. ERSKINE CLARKE (Ed.) *Children's Prize*, 1873

The Agonies of Death

After a while his eyes half shut, and he fell into the agonies of death.

Death – even the death of those whose souls are redeemed – is a dreadful sight; for the sinful body struggles hard with it. Satan then does his worst; but it is written, 'He that is with us is stronger than he that is against us;' and He will surely deliver those whom He hath purchased with his precious blood, even from the power of death and hell.

After several convulsive pangs, little Charles stretched himself: he breathed slower, and slower, and slower; then, fetching a deep sigh, his features became fixed in death. Nurse, who had come into the room some time before, perceiving that the soul of the dear child was departed, came up to the bedside, and gently closed the eyes, and bound up with a handkerchief the mouth of the corpse; and having laid the arms and feet straight upon the bed, she stepped back to wipe away the tears that were running fast down her cheeks. All this while no one spoke, but all stood silently looking on the features of the dear child as they settled in death. After a few moments, Mr Somers gave notice that he was going to pray, and every one knelt down around the bed. Mr Somers' prayer was very short, but it was very solemn: he first gave God thanks for the happy departure of the dear child, now with

A family death-bed scene

Christ his Redeemer; and, secondly, he earnestly prayed that
God would, in his appointed time, grant unto all then present
an equally happy death. His prayer finished with these words:
'May we die the death of the righteous, and may our latter
end be like his!'

MRS SHERWOOD *The History of the Fairchild Family,*
1880 Edition

Recollections of Corpses

I think it was only this last baby whose little wax-like corpse
I saw. The darkened room, the little coffin covered with grey
cloth, the closed eyes, the soft flannel dress tied at the wrists
with wite satin ribbon, those little marble hands – Oh how
present it all is even now to my memory! It was the first time
I had seen a corpse, but I have seen many since – some among
the poor; I do not like to shrink from the sight, and it is often
a pleasure to the poor mother, and even to the widow, that you
should see the orderly and neat arrangements they have strug-
gled to make; turn not away, it is humbling, painful, but it
will help to lift your heart to heaven.
And yet I once gazed on a corpse which I had rather not have
seen, so vivid and painful has the impression been. A young
person, a distant relation, who lived with the deceased lady,
had accepted my offer of calling to see her, an offer though
not intimate, circumstances rendered it fitting that I should
make, and as I rose to leave her, she said, 'Will you walk into
the other room?' I thought she might feel hurt if I declined to
do so, and we went in. There, in a rich coffin, lay the poor
decaying body, decked as in life – false hair, the blond cap,
the costly gown, the satin shoes – Oh it was a revolting sight.
'Did she wish it?' I said, 'O yes,' said her young relation, with a
mournful but calm look, 'I hope I have done all she could have
wished.' . . .

PRIMOGENITA *Recollections of Childhood,* 1840

THE
WIDENING WORLD

Domestic, charitable and evangelical sorties were made into shops, streets and the houses of the poor. Even so close to the fortress of home lurked such dangers as intemperance and cruelty to animals. Falling into temptation was shown to lead to inevitable punishment. There were ethical as well as religious lessons to be learnt in the outside world.

Further afield, but growing more accessible with new and quicker means of transport and communications, beckoned the gas-lit fairyland of big towns and cities. Zoos, circuses, exhibitions, waxworks, museums, public parks and gardens were broadening experiences for respectable children guided by adults. When such places were open on Sundays, thanks to the National Sunday League, the working classes emerged from their dark satanic mills to share them. These people were, generally speaking, no threat to juvenile readers. Their presence added to the atmosphere. On the whole the mutinous proletariat never appeared on young horizons. The real danger was the corrupting influence of low commercial entertainment. The seaside and countryside were described with rural and feudal nostalgia: places for refreshment of mind and body. In the same spirit artists were painting landscapes for urban parents to compensate for industrial squalor. Even so it was less a romantic idyll than a visual record, like pressed ferns and collected fossils. Excursions must be useful and educative as well as enjoyable.

'Abroad', to children, must have been a baffling mixture of magnificence and horror. The Great Exhibition at the Crystal Palace in 1851 showed the exotic splendours of the 'Art and Industry of All Nations.' They had learnt about patriotism, about the Empire and British supremacy at their mother's knee. The military imagery of hymns taught them about the glories of professional soldiering. On the other hand Abroad, they were told, was bristling with dangers, ranging from the Catholics across the channel to hideous heathen practices in India.

Aristocratic heads were rolling in Europe. Slaves had been rescued, but their freedom looked blacker than their bondage. Missionaries were moral heroes, but explorers were suffering terrible fates. It may have been the thin end of the wedge for this generation whose complacency ended with the Boer Wars. It was a challenging world, without apathy or cynicism. But it was still the world of the Plain Man, whose children must always be brought down to earth..

War

I hate thee, sanguinary war!
And hold thee up to view,
That all may see thy frightful form,
And learn to hate thee too.

I care not who knows the fact, but I had rather talk about war for a whole day than engage in it for a single hour. I hold that to be the worst occupation in the world, wherein a man is required, with provocation, to break another's head, and cut another's throat. It is a black blot on the forehead of an individual, and of a nation, unnecessarily to go to war. They who can shed blood without remorse, must be content to lose their own without pity.

A friend of mine, who is a most excellent painter, shewed me a capital picture of a battle. There were gallant fellows represented therein dressed in gay regimentals, and mounted on fine horses, cutting down all before them. The painting was full of spirit; you might fancy that you heard the roll of the drums, and the flourish of the tumpets. The sun shone on the field, and the unfurled colours seemed almost to flap, to and fro, in the battle-blast. 'This is a glorious scene,' said my friend the painter, 'and enough to make one sigh to be a soldier! It is a fine thing to be dressed in scarlet, to gain a victory, and to wear around one's brow a wreath of deathless glory!'

Now, as my friend had treated me with a sight of his valuable painting, I felt disposed to acquit myself of the obligation by shewing him a few sketches of my own. The first was that of a fine young soldier, in gay regimentals, writhing on the field of battle, with a bayonet through his back, and a part of his jaw shot away. The second represented a horse-soldier, lying on the ground, whose head had been cleft by the stroke of a broadsword, and whose mangled face was crushed by the iron hoof of his own charger. The third exhibited a scene of carnage, where colours, and drums, and trumpets, were more than half hidden by the dead and dying. The fourth was a sketch of an aged woman, oppressed with grief on hearing the tidings of the death of her dear boy in battle. The fifth, the outline of a grey-headed father, cursing, in the frenzy of his affliction, the horrors of cruel war, which had just drained away the life-blood of his only son. And the sixth, a spirited sketch of a recruiting sergeant, gaily dressed, smiling, and holding up a purse of gold, while, in the distance, was seen the weather-beaten figure of an old soldier with a bundle at his back, stumping along on two wooden legs, and a stick in each hand. 'Oh!' said I to my friend, 'these are glorious scenes, enough to make one sigh to be a soldier! It is a fine thing to be dressed in scarlet to gain a victory, and to wear around one's brow a wreath of deathless glory!'

CARLTON BRUCE *The Boy's Friend*

To be a Soldier

'Why would you like to be a soldier?' said the questioner.
'Oh!' returned Jack. 'I should like to have a sword, and a gun, and a cocked hat, and a plume of feathers, and to *march*. Lend me your crutch, grandfather,' he continued, snatching it from his side over the gouty toe, which made the old man wince a bit. 'Shoulder arms! Order arms!' – ('Oh, my toe!') – 'Up guards and at 'em! – Stand at *ease*!'
'I wish I could,' replied the old gentleman: 'that would be a happy thing for me. Now you stand at ease, will you, and just hear what I have to say. You would like to be a soldier, would you?'
'Yes, I would,' said Jack.
'Well,' replied the old gentleman, 'it's a noble profession, and it embraces honourable men in every grade, and it is a glory to fight for one's king and country. But war is a dreadful game! – bullets and bombs; blood and carnage; limbs lopped off here, and heads there; blown up at one place, blown over in another; cut up, and cut down; trampled on by charging squadrons; pounded into a mummy. It's all very fine to hear the drums beat, and for the flags to wave over you, and the cannon to fire on account of the victory when you are dead. Have you thought of all this?'
'No,' said Jack, 'I don't think I have quite.'

WILLIAM MARTIN (Ed.) *Peter Parley's Own*
Favourite Story Book

The Steam Boat.

George is Lazy

He that gathereth in summer is a wise son; but he that sleepeth in harvest is a son that causeth shame.

Proverbs X. v. 5.

The sun is very hot in the sky, and George is lazy and has laid down on the wheat, and fallen fast asleep. I am afraid such an idle, self-indulgent boy will never do any good for himself; and that his father will be quite ashamed of such a 'poor thing' of a son. If boys will not bear a little discomfort they will never grow into brave and prosperous men. I am sure this lazy boy will never make a man like Dr. Livingstone, who bears the heat of Africa that he may do good; nor like brave Captain McClintock, who did not fear the cold North Pole. No wonder that (as God's Book tells us) his father will feel ashamed ot him! Do not be like him. Learn to 'Endure hardness as a good soldier of Christ.'

ANON   *The Proverbs of Solomon*

What a Child May Do

A little boy in London, who attended a Sabbath school, having occasion every Lord's-day to go through a certain court, observed a shop open for the sale of goods. Shocked at such a profanation, he considered whether it was possible for him to do any thing to prevent it. He determined to leave a tract on the 'Lord's-day,' as he passed the shop in the course of the week. He did so; and on the following Sabbath observed that the shop was shut up. Surprised at this, he stopped, and considered whether it would be the effect of the tract he had left. He ventured to knock gently at the door, when a woman within, thinking it was a customer, answered aloud, 'You cannot have any thing, we don't sell on the Sunday.' Encouraged by what he had heard, the little boy still begged for admittance; when the woman, recollecting his voice, said, 'Come in, my dear little fellow: it was you that left the tract here against Sabbath breaking; and it alarmed me so, that I did not dare to keep my shop open any longer, and I am determined never to do so again while I live.'

ANON   *The Children's Friend*, January 1865

Mr Bianconi's Opinion

At the Meeting of the British Association in Dublin, in August 1857, Mr Charles Bianconi, of Cashel, read a paper relative to his extensive car establishment, after which a gentleman stated that at Pickford's, the great English carriers, they could not work a horse economically more than ten miles a-day, and wished to hear Mr Bianconi's opinion on the subject. Mr Bianconi stated, he found, by experience, he could *better* work a horse eight miles a-day for *six* days in the week, than six miles a-day for *seven* days in the week. By not working on a Sunday, he effected a *saving of twelve per cent*. This statement elicited loud applause.

Mr Bianconi's opinion on this point is of the highest authority; for although the extension of railways in the land has thrown thirty-seven of his vehicles out of employ, which daily ran 2,446 miles, still he has over nine hundred horses, working sixty-seven conveyances, which daily travel 4,244 miles: it is also founded on the result of forty-three years' experience. Thus it appears that, if men will only act from selfish motives, 'in keeping God's commandments there is an exceeding great reward.'

ANON   *A Mother's Lessons on Kindness to Animals*

A Cruel Reaper Punished

In several parts of North Wales, the labouring classes are in the habit of going down to Shropshire, and other counties of England, to do the harvesting work, and afterwards returning home, in time for reaping in their own neighbourhood.

It was in one of these excursions, that a young man, who had given himself up to intemperance, was returning home in a drunken frolic. He espied a poor donkey feeding on the roadside; he advanced towards it, and with his reaping-hook struck it across the spine, and left the poor thing in agonies to die. Was he unpunished? No.

Soon after this deed of cruelty, whilst at work blasting stones, a premature explosion took place, from the effects of which he was obliged to have his arm cut off. He also lost his sight, and spent the remainder of his days in the Union workhouse.

ANON   *A Mother's Lessons on Kindness to Animals*

A tale of the sea

The Cold-Water Boy

'Well, sir! What will you take?' said the landlord, who was always ready to be pleased with anything a little out of the common order. 'A brandy punch, mint julep, sherry cobbler, or a hot whisky punch? All capital drinks!'

There were two or three old tippling customers in the bar-room, idling their time away, instead of being at their work. Here was a little novelty for them; and they gathered around the newcomer, pleased as could be at the prospect of something to break in upon the dullness of the hour. If one of them thought of the dangerous course the lad was apparently entering, it did not occur to his mind, at the same time, that it was his duty to warn him of his folly. All felt like having some sport out of the boy.

'Try a sherry cobbler,' said one, speaking up quickly. 'It's first-rate.'

'No, no,' said another. 'Nothing like hot whisky punch. Try that.'

And one pulled him one way and one another, while the landlord said, with mock gravity – he was enjoying the scene wonderfully.

'Come – come, sirs! Let the gentleman choose for himself. I reckon he knows what's what, as well as any of you. Now, sir,' addressing Frank, 'which will you take?'

Frank had not been in the least confused by all the hub-bub his appearance had created; and, as soon as he could get a chance to order what he wanted, said, with the utmost coolness –

'I'll take a glass of Adam's ale, if you please, landlord.'

It was a little curious to see how the laugh began gradually to change to the 'other side of the mouth,' the moment Frank said this.

'Oh! Adam's ale,' returned the landlord, doing his best to keep up the little farce he was acting. 'Yes – very good drink that – only a little too weak.' And he poured Frank out a glass of pure, sparkling water, which the lad drank off with the air of one who enjoyed it.

'How does it taste?' inquired one of the tipplers, thinking still to throw the laugh off upon Frank.

'Try a little, won't you?' said the boy, with a serious face. 'I'm sure you'll like the taste. It makes you feel good all over; it hasn't a particle of headache or fever in it.'

'Indeed! So you're a young teetotaller,' remarked Hartley.

The Cold-Water Boy

'I'm a cold-water boy,' said Frank, as he stepped back from the bar. 'And, in return for your compliment, this morning, invite you to join our army. We'll make you captain.'
Frank did not say this pertly, nor impudently, as most boys would have done, but with such grave good-humour, that it was impossible for anyone to be offended. The landlord was taken entirely by surprise; and, before he could recover himself and renew the attack, Frank bade him good morning, and retired.

T. S. ARTHUR *Our Little Harry*, 1855

Selling lavender and umbrellas

Virtuous Female Intercourse

Do not try, then, to get out of the way of female intercourse. I have known young men avoid what they ought to have rejoiced in, and thus lose its beneficial influence. They were, indeed, sensible of not being quite suitable company for anything delicate or refined, and they sunk, rather than rose, on the occasion. This was not to their improvement, but quite the contrary.

THOMAS TEGG *A Present For An Apprentice*, 1848

Above: Buckingham Palace – 'now the principal royal
residence in town.'
Below: A spring outing
Both from *The Pleasant Verse and Prose Story Book*

Dangers of the Playhouse

Then, there are the playhouses. A large proportion of young
men in cities take their first decisive step towards ruin across
the threshold of the theatre. . . .

It is not contended that no young man can ever go to the
theatre without receiving great and apparent injury; but it is
always dangerous, and to multitudes it is the highway to ruin.
I have not time to enlarge upon the numerous evils to which
play-going exposes you; but it is an outlay of *money* which few
young men can well afford. Hence individuals have thus been
fatally tempted to obtain means in an unlawful way – perhaps
by defrauding, or by purloining from their employers – in
order to support the indulgence. It is not the *play*, but the
playhouse, which is to be dreaded, and through which a really
play-going youth is almost sure to fall a victim to licentious-
ness.

THOMAS TEGG   *A Present For An Apprentice*, 1848

The Little Tract Girl

Who is that little girl I see every Sunday morning pass my
house? She carries in her hand a small bundle of books: what
can they be about? If I meet her in an hour's time, there are
not so many in the parcel as at first: what does she do with
them? I should like to know a little more about this little girl.
Such were my thoughts; and you shall now hear what I found
out about her.

It was on a fine morning in June, and at the hour when
children are seen on their way to the Sunday-school, that I saw
the little girl come down the street. A sweet smile was on her
face. I felt quite sure that she had a happy heart, and I could
not but hope that she was one of Christ's dear lambs.

I passed over to the opposite side of the street, lest I should
be noticed. She had gone only a few steps, when she met a
little boy and his sister, who either knew little about Sunday
as a holy day, or cared not to keep it. She stopped, and untied
a piece of ribbon that was round her bundle; then drawing out
two tracts, she gave them to the children, saying, 'I hope I
shall not see you playing in the street next Sunday.'

On turning a corner at a short distance, I heard the voice of an aged woman: 'Here comes our little tract girl.' The child stopped again, and the old woman soon came to the door on crutches, for she was lame. 'I am glad to see you again, my darling,' said she: 'I have lived on that sweet tract you gave me last sabbath all through the week.' The little girl, with a smile and a few modest words, put two other tracts in her hand, and then bidding the aged woman 'good-bye', passed on with nimble feet.

ANON *The Child's Companion and Juvenile Instructor*, 1860

Little Shoeblack

When the little Shoeblack saw them coming, he began to say: 'Clean your boots, gentlemen? Clean your boots, gentlemen?' louder than ever, for he saw there was a chance of custom for him. And sure enough the two boys stopped; and first one put his feet on the box and had his boots cleaned, and then the other. And as for the little Shoeblack, he rubbed and rubbed away till his face was as red as his jacket, with the work, and the boys' toes must have felt red-hot. But he made their boots shine like polished ebony, and so they went away very well satisfied. As the little Shoeblack got a penny from each of them, I have no doubt he was well satisfied too.
This little boy once prowled about the streets, hungry and ragged. At last some kind people, who pitied him and all stray boys like him, thought of a plan by which they might benefit him. They opened a 'Ragged School', and all little ragged boys were invited to come. He came among the rest; and as he was willing to learn, and showed himself grateful for any kindness, after a time he was dressed in the red flannel jacket, and the box and brushes were given to him, and he went out to earn his living. What a happy little boy he was then, and how proud of being trusted! If he goes on as well as I hope he will there will be better work for him to do soon.

ANON *Pictures from the Street*

Nurse Griffin's Levee

'Come here,' said nurse; 'there, stoop down – I'm not going to bite you, girl. No child will ever respect or mind you while you tell so many stories. Children hear, see, and understand more than you think. Whenever you tell a lie to a child, or before a child, that child will never again believe you. Be what you try to make your mistress believe you *are*, and you will then be able to manage the children.'

Of course, Nurse Griffin had a word of reproof for all the nursemaids in the square, and sundry kind words to all the children. There was soon a crowd of little people round her – a perfect levee; they all knew her. She was the frequent umpire in their disputes, the mediator with papa, or mamma, as the case might be. She was seldom cross, and even when tantalised and teased, very, very seldom unjust; and there is nothing that children more highly appreciate than justice. It was a pretty group; Nurse Griffin, so stately and erect, and so scrupulously well dressed, for her station, in the greyest of gowns, the whitest of caps and bonnets, upon which no soil was ever seen, and a delicate, transparent, white shawl, gracefully draped over her shoulders. To her, the world was a succession of babies, and nearly all the bright, sparkling young things that gathered round her, after she had taken her seat beneath the foliage of those grand old trees, had been babies on her arm immediately after their birth. Nurse looked upon them with almost a maternal feeling; they had been *hers*, and, as she loved to say, 'Bless their hearts, they never forgot her.'

'Oh, nurse, let me look at the new baby,' petitioned a wild-eyed girl.

'No, Miss Sumners; the last time I let you look at Mrs Tymison's sweetest treasure, you behaved as I thought no young lady as ever I carried in its beautiful long clothes could behave to a precious innocent – you tried to give it snuff! Go away, Miss Sumners.'

'Well, me, nurse; may I look?' cried another.

'Yes, Miss Grace Nugent, and welcome.'

'Oh, nurse, what a potty-paddy darling – and its fubsey-bubsey hands – and its dear blue eyes!'

'Black, you mean, miss,' said Nurse Griffin; 'that's my opinion.'

S. C. HALL AND OTHERS *The Story Garden*, 1876

Crossing the Brook.

In Service

When, on leaving this place, Bessy paid a visit to her parents, and in her very best apparel, a tall comely young woman, made her first appearance at church, all her old companions looked upon her as a person whose acquaintance would be very creditable to them. Her mother too, with a very pardonable pride, when the service was over, stopped on purpose that the clergyman and his wife might see her.

A proud and happy woman was she, when they acknowledged her deep curtsey and that of the daughter with a very gracious smile, of which she gave half the credit to Bessy's respectable appearance. The squire's lady too waited to see them pass, and then turned and spoke to her handsome daughter, something which Mrs Brown was sure, in her own mind, was to Bessy's advantage – and the poor woman walked home, the happiest mother in the whole congregation. 'I always thought she would be a credit to us,' she said to herself; 'such a tidy, notable girl! – I hope Mary, and Jane, and little Sarah will turn out as well!'

The next day, to the great joy of Bessy's mother, the clergyman's pony-chaise stopped at their cottage door, and in a few minutes his lady entered to make inquiries respecting her. If she could have a good character from her last place, she said she could offer her a situation in her own family. Bessy's good conscience assured her, in a moment, all would be right; and blushing, and full of ill-concealed joy, she thanked the kind lady for the offer a thousand times. A favourable character was soon received from her late mistress, and in two weeks' time the dream of Bessy's childhood was realised, and she and her personal property, now occupying two tolerably large paper trunks, besides the little oaken chest before mentioned, were removed to the beautiful parsonage. Here she lived five years, a happy and respectable servant, fulfilling every duty, and with a conscience void of offence; and at the end of that time only left it to be married to her fellow-servant, the gardener, as steady and industrious a young man as even Mrs Brown herself could desire for her dutiful daughter.

MARY HOWITT *Tales in Prose*

Nothing Like Work

The working classes of this country are an honour to it, for they are fond of labour, and are patient under poverty, even though they are ground down with it to the bone. The English labourer, who was once our country's boast and pride, has sunk, and is sinking, to the lowest depths of indigence, and little more cared for than a pig or a donkey. The artisan is better looked upon; he is paid better, and fed better, and he knows better what is proper for himself. The time will come when he is better cared for than he is now, not through the hands of charity, but through his own exertions. But it is not for poor old Peter Parley to whine or grumble even for himself or for others. He has worked hard, and still works, and will continue to work till the last.

There is nothing like work, my boys; and it is work, not money, that makes the man, who increases the wealth of the country, from the east to the west, from the north to the south, from the mine, from the mill, and the little stream that prattles by its side, to its ceaseless clatter, and whence the gleaners come and go, and mingle their harvest song with is constant melody. And not from mines and mills only does the voice of labour proceed; the blacksmith's forge and the mighty clang of hammers speak of labour; the windlass and the crane, the pile-rammer, the axe, the pickaxe, the spade, the crowbar, the chisel, and even the nimble little gimlet, all have a tale to tell

LOVELY SPRING.

of work, and to justify the great blessing of God to man, who
was made to work in the Garden of Eden, and not left even
in the bower of paradise to lead a life of idleness.
So let us labour. Let us begin early; we are to labour at school,
and work away at our tasks to master the difficulties of
grammar, and to 'grind gerunds' in the mill of the academy.
Let us work, ay, from our very infancy; let us play too: yet
play should not be idleness, but effort; let us beat the ball,
knock down the wicket, vault over the ditch, fly the kite, spin
the top, or shoot the marble with spirit and skill, and so work
away even in play.
All these are pleasing sights; but of all the pleasing sights con-

SWEET SUMMER.

nected with the life of a working man, is to see him about the
hour of noon coming to some cool shady place to meet his wife
and children, who have brought him his dinner, and who sit
down to share it with him, while, in the very ecstasy of fatherly
love, he takes his youngest boy and holds him up trium-
phantly over his head, while at the same time he gives God
thanks in his heart for blessings now realised. It is a pretty
picture, and surpasses in interest the grand battles of war,
where thousands of poor fellows bite the dust, and are cut to
pieces by one another's swords and cannons.

WILLIAM MARTIN (Ed.) *Peter Parley's Annual*, 1867

Hopping

The party at the Rectory, and the other still larger party at the old Court, suited each other, or, as Harry D'Eyncourt said, 'dove-tailed' perfectly; and, perhaps, few happier days were ever known by any of them than the fortnight spent in Mr Chester's hop garden at Fairdown that year.

Early breakfasts were the order of the day; and before breakfast, a constant communication was kept up between the two houses, by means of flying messages carried by Charlie, Harry, Arthur, Fanny, and Martha.

To express the fulness of their delight during the fortnight, would be impossible. Harry and Arthur were entrusted with the care of all the stools, cushions, cloaks, shawls, coats, parasols, umbrellas, etc., that were used by the party every day. These they put into a light truck, drawn by a Newfoundland dog (the equipage was their own contrivance), that carried them up every morning to the Windmill hill, on the side of which the hop garden lay, and they brought them back in the same way every evening.

As soon as they had arranged seats for all the ladies as comfortably as they could, and had caused some of the labourers to bring the requisite number of bins to that corner of the garden, the two boys would go back again with their dog-cart, after adorning it with fresh hop-corealties, and bring Fanny and Martha in it, who rode along in state, carrying the books, and drawing, and needlework, entrusted to them by the elder folks.

By the time they reached the scene of operations, the Rectory party would generally arrive; Laura and Alice Merle wore large coarse straw hats on this occasion, which Frank and Henry Danvers would wreath with hops, preparatory to the day's work. Mr and Mrs D'Eyncourt, and Mr James Danvers (who was writing a poem about the working classes), would saunter away to all parts of the garden, greeting the busy hoppers, who had been at work there ever since four o'clock. Some of these were the Fairdown village folks; but most of them were very poor people from London, who go down every autumn into Kent and Surrey, with their wives and children, seeking employment in the hop-gardens. When the weather was fine, as it was this year, the change was very advantageous for them.

How the poor, pale children, who are pent up in London alleys all the year, enjoy a hopping season! see them play about during their brief meal times! hear them laugh over their bins, throwing the beautiful wreaths at each other! This was a great source of pleasure to Arthur and Fanny, whose hearts had often been moved to compassion by the sight of London children, who had never been into the country in their lives. Here, in the course of a week, their thin white faces would begin to get plump and rosy. As Arthur told Fanny 'It was a great pity hopping could not last all the year round.'

MISS WINNARD   *Fanny and Arthur*

The Entente Cordiale

'And what a number of things I can see, papa!' cried Rose. 'Look at the red curtains, and the crimson flags. Look at the white marble statues, the bronze images, the golden vases, and the sparkling fountains! How light and fairy-like the building is! how pretty the stripes of blue on the columns, and what brilliant colours there are on the tapestries! Then, look at the crowds of black hats, and the bright yellow bonnets moving about. Two men with *red* hats are coming down the aisle in the midst of the black ones – there is a Turk with his white turban – a Frenchman wearing a cap – and there is another patch of red, made by four soldiers. How they move on in a thick stream near the Transept, and pass the crystal fountain! See how some are loitering and looking – some are sitting – other standing – and other lounging about doing—'
'Stop, Rose,' said Henry, 'listen! There is someone playing the French organ! He is playing *God Save the Queen*.'

P: Ah, how beautiful that sound is! and how pleasant the thought, that *God Save the Queen* is being played by a *Frenchman*!

'Yes,' said Henry, 'and he begins by saying, "God bless *our* gracious Queen." '

P: And all those people from many nations, whom you see mingled together in one crowd – may they be able to sing with him! Let them sing the new words of the National Anthem, which were made to be sung in better days:

And not this land alone,
But be thy mercies known
From shore to shore!
Lord, make the nations see
That men should brothers be,
And form one family,
The wide world o'er.

ROSE: Ah, I wish that they would all sing that!

P: Perhaps they will one day. But it is now getting rather late; we must return home.

ANON   *Little Henry's Holiday at the Great Exhibition*

Hook Swinging

Not long ago there lived in India a young woman, who was a servant in an officer's family. Her husband was one of the horsekeepers in the Indian army. They were both heathen, but they served their master faithfully. For a long time they had no child, and when at last she had a little boy she thought that her gods had sent it in answer to her prayers. But you know, though she did not, that the idols had no power to do anything she asked them. She wished to show her gratitude to them; but you will hardly believe what a terrible thing she thought would please them. About this time was held a grand festival in honour of the goddess Siva. One of the things done at this festival was called 'hook-swinging.' This poor young woman said she would be one of those to be swung on the hooks. As soon as her master and mistress heard what she was going to do, they tried very hard to persuade her not to do it;

248

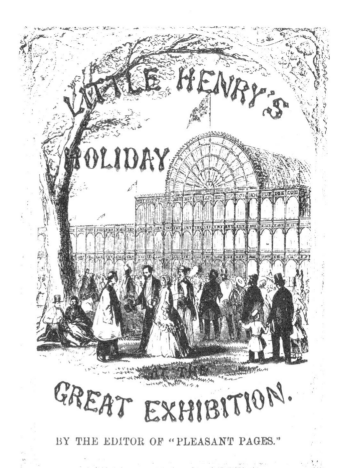

LITTLE HENRY'S HOLIDAY AT THE GREAT EXHIBITION.

BY THE EDITOR OF "PLEASANT PAGES."

LONDON: HOULSTON & STONEMAN,
AND ALL BOOKSELLERS.

Price 2s 6d

Title page

and they told her husband that if he allowed her to take a part in this horrid rite, they would not keep him or his wife as their servants any longer. But no one could persuade her to give it up. The officer and his wife were very sorry to lose their servants.

At last the day of the feast came. I must tell you how this painful 'hook-swinging' was done. Two large hooks, like meat-hooks, were stuck into this poor woman's back. The hooks were fastened to an iron pole, which was fixed into a cart. When the cart was drawn on, the hooks swung round and round, and in this way the woman was carried through the town. Crowds of people followed, shouting and singing. She bore the dreadful pain most bravely, but it is sad to think her courage was shown in a way that could do nobody any good. . . .

You have now heard of the sad manner in which a poor heathen mother showed her thankfulness, and of the far better way in which Hannah, who worshipped the only true God, showed her gratitude to Him, when He had granted her desire. There are many other heathens, besides this poor woman, who think their idols are cruel, and that they must do cruel things to please them. Our Missionaries are gone to teach them that the only God who can hear and answer prayer, is a kind and merciful Father, and wishes people only to love and serve Him, and to teach their children to love Him also.

ANON   *The Church Missionary Juvenile Instructor*, 1865

Dreadful Cannibalism

In the Island of Hayti a man and his wife stole one of their own nieces, a girl about eight years of age, strangled her, flayed her, cut her up, cooked her, and then devoured her, offering the blood to their god – the snake.
Never let us forget that 'the dark places of the earth' are *still* 'the habitations of cruelty.'

ANON   *The Church Missionary Juvenile Instructor*, 1865

Niger Mission

The Rev J. C. Taylor, the native Missionary, gives a lamentable account of the state of heathen Onitsha. Mr Taylor writes:
I have seen canoes from the upper part of the river brought down to Onitsha with slaves of both sexes. Since my return to my station, oftentimes my heart has ached to see a canoe-load of human beings down at the landing-place. The wealthy purchase them, and keep them either for their own funeral rites, or for those of their relatives. One morning a member of my church came up to me with tears in her eyes, telling me that a chief was trying to purchase two little girls from a canoe which had just landed here, to offer as sacrifice to his deceased son. She earnestly begged me to rescue them. I sent the woman to fetch the girls to me. When she reached the mart the chief had purchased one of them, and was bargaining for the other. She paid her price, and brought her to me. Oh what a sight to behold! She was shivering with cold, in perfect

Africans' first sight of a Looking-glass in the Hut of Dr. Livingstone.

nudity, and emaciated through hunger. She was about seven years of age. Her price was 62,400 cowries, equal to £31 18s. She is now placed in school under the fostering care of the 'Coral Fund,' and has been baptised by the name of Amelia Westcott. The other was sacrificed at the grave.

ANON The Church Missionary Juvenile Instructor, 1865

It Is Called New Zealand

It is called New Zealand, and those funny-looking people are called New Zealanders. They talk a language which you could not understand, and they are, many of them, very fierce and cruel, for they do not know that it is wrong to fight and quarrel, to hate and provoke one another. So there are often very dreadful wars in New Zealand between the different tribes, who fight most willingly whenever their chiefs choose to quarrel with each other; and every man in the army tries to kill the greatest number of the enemies, because then he is thought very brave and praised very much.

Do you know why it is that the New Zealanders are so cruel? It is because they do not know and love Jesus Christ, who is the Prince of Peace; they are the servants of the wicked one, who the Bible tells us is like a roaring lion, going about seeking whom he may devour. . . .

So when they came to England, and had seen many wonderful things which they had never even heard of before, had ridden in the train, had visited the large places where cloth, and china, paper, pins and needles are made; when they had seen all this, what do you think they said they liked best? Why they said, 'We do not care to see the English gaieties, we do not always like those things which we expected to like; we like to see the things the English people make, but what we like best of all is to see the English people worship God.'

But there was one thing that these good New Zealanders did not like in England. They were very much grieved when they saw people buying and selling in the streets on Sunday. They knew that it was God's holy day, and that He has commanded us to do no work on that day, but to spend it in worshipping Him, in reading about Him, and in telling others about what He has done; and so one Sunday, when a woman came to their house to sell strawberries, they were very sorry, and one of them said to her, in his broken English, 'What for you do this?' And when she began to make excuses, he pointed up to heaven, and told her that God who lived above the sky would see and punish her.

Do you not think that she must have been very much ashamed to find that this poor man who had only heard a little while before about the love of God, and about his soul, should be so much better than she was who had lived all her life in England, where there are so many Bibles and so many churches and ministers, that nobody can say they could not find out the way to heaven?

ANON   *True Stories for Little People*, 1865

A Chapter for Young America

I have a few words for the private ear of Young America. These are not for the girls. I have something private for them when I see them; but they will please to skip this page, and say nothing about it. This is for the boys.

And now, my young friends, let me give you a piece of advice: don't spit, if you can help it! If you must spit, do it privately. Never spit on a carpet; never spit on a floor. Never do this in a private house; never do it in a hotel; never do it in a steam boat; never do it in a rail-car; never in a church or meeting house. You may not know it; but spitting is offensive to well-bred people, and if you would not disgust them, do it always as privately as possible.

It is true that some people who imagine themselves to be well-bred, are in the habit of spitting right and left, as if it were an accomplishment. I have seen tall walking, tall talking Americans, young and old, do this. I have seen them do it in the halls, and reading-rooms, and parlors of the fine hotels in Broadway. Nay, I have seen them do it in the Representatives'

ABOVE *African scholars*

253

Hall, and the Senate room, and the room of the Supreme Court, at Washington. Nevertheless, this is a very vulgar and offensive habit, and I am sorry to say, it is exclusively an American habit. In no other part of the world do persons, pretending to be gentlemen, defile halls, and parlors, and carpets, and furniture, with human slaver.

I remember once, while travelling in Italy, to have been in a steamboat, on the Mediterranean. It was a beautiful day, and as we were running along the coast of Sardinia, all the passengers were on deck. Some were English, some French, some Italians, and a few were Americans. Among the latter was a young man, having the easy air of our rich countrymen abroad – seated in a chair upon the deck, by himself. He sat looking forth upon the water, and occasionally dropping his spittle between his feet, on the deck. He repeated this till he had made quite a puddle, which swayed to and fro with the lurches of the vessel. At last it broke loose, and flowed in a stream across the deck. 'Look there,' said a young Englishman to his companion, 'do you see the *American Autograph!*' Young America did not hear this; had he heard it, he would not have understood it. Even if it had been said to him that he should not spit before people, I fear he might have resented it as an encroachment upon his natural rights; for I must tell you that he chewed tobacco, and what can a man do – who chews tobacco – but spit?

While I am on the subject of tobacco, let me say a word which I wish all my young friends to remember. I say it after long observation and due reflection. *No man can be a gentleman, who chews tobacco!* The reason is, that it defiles the mouth, it defiles the breath, and it begets a constant necessity for an issue of black saliva, from the mouth. To be a gentleman, is to be clean, personally: to chew tobacco, is to be filthy personally. So, whoever wishes to be a gentleman, let him not chew tobacco.

I beg to repeat that this is a private chapter, only whispered in the ear of my young countrymen, for whose welfare and prosperity, I feel a deep interest. All others, I trust, will have the delicacy never to mention the subject.

S. G. GOODRICH *Juvenile Forget-Me-Not*, 1858

Rowing to the Tower, from *The Town and Country
Toy Book*

Henry and Seth

He spent two months in New York, and was as much gratified as Henry had been by his two months in Litchfield county. The boys went about together, and Henry enjoyed things he was familiar with, over again, as he now perceived them through Seth's greedy eyes and ears. They went down to the wharves, and saw the shipping and the steamers; they went to the foundries, and heard and saw the deafening clang of making boilers and other machinery. They went to Barnum's Museum several days in succession, and looked with admiring wonder on the strange things there gathered together. They went into Trinity Church, and Seth was amazed at its grandeur and magnificence. Accustomed as he was to a light, airy, country meeting-house, his senses were a little dazzled with the mixture of purple fire and brassy gold, which was diffused through the stained windows of this superb edifice; but he was too polite to speak of it. . . .

And the two boys went to Harpers' book store, which seemed like a city of itself. In one place there were persons drawing pictures on smooth pieces of wood, and these were to be engraved and printed in books. There were some persons setting up types, and some were printing with machines, and some were binding books, and some were packing books in boxes to be sent to Boston, and Philadelphia, and New Orleans, and all over the world. The two boys were introduced into a room where was an elderly gentleman, whom they were told was James Harper, the 'Head of the House', and Seth thought that, next to Solomon, he must be the greatest man that had been heard of yet. Here they saw Mr Abbott, who writes the beautiful books for children. He was a pleasant looking person, and Seth was rather taken aback to discover that one who had written so much was only a man, and looked very much like deacon Smith!

From Harpers', the boys went to other book stores. Barnes', Derby & Jackson's, Wiley & Halsted's, Francis', and others. At last, they came to Appletons'. Before entering, Seth looked up at the building, and his idea was, that it must be Solomon's Temple. When he got in, the loftiness of the ceilings, and the depth of the aisles – the sides all garnished with books in every variety of bindings – have him such a sudden stretch of intellect as almost to disturb his understanding. He, however, soon recovered, and spent some happy hours in looking over the various publications which were kindly shown to

him by one of the clerks. This whole scene at Appletons' made a deep impression on Seth, and his greatest ambition, and highest hope, is one day to be a clerk in this establishment. I recommend him to the good will of the proprietors.

S. G. GOODRICH   *Juvenile Forget-Me-Not*, 1858

The Negro Slave

In a country a long way off, there lived, in a poor hut, a Negro woman and her child. The Negroes have black skins.

This woman was a slave. We have no slaves here, but in the country of which I speak, where the people read the same Bible, and speak the same language as we do, strange and sad to tell, they have slaves. They buy and sell Negroes there just as you may have seen horses and cattle bought and sold in a market. This poor Negro woman had been sold to a cruel master. She might not leave him and go to another, as a servant may do in our country, if she is not happy; for her master had bought her, had given money for her, to a man, a long time since, and he called her his own. But who gave that man leave to sell her? Not God, for he has made of one blood all those that dwell on the earth. He made the Negro, as well as the white man; and he loves all that he has made. So you see that no one could have given the man leave to sell the poor Negro, for she belonged to no one, but to the God who made her, and that God has said, 'Thou shalt not steal.'

MRS THOMAS GELDART   *The Nursery Guide*, 1850

A Very Kind Officer

If you never thanked the great God for making you a little free, white child living in England, where the Bible is read, and people know the way to heaven; if you never felt very thankful for all this, I should like you to go to some of those places in West Africa where the poor black slaves live; and when you saw how much they suffer, I am sure you would say,

'Ah! I am so glad I am not a little black child.'

Shall I tell you what happened a little while ago to an English captain who was sailing in his ship near the coast of West Africa? He had been sent out by the Queen of England to try and take the ships which carry the poor slaves away from Africa to sell them in other countries, and as he was a very kind man, I am sure he must have been very anxious to meet some of these ships, that he might be able to set the poor blacks free.

Well, it was a very dark night, and the rain was falling fast, when the man who was on deck saw a ship not far off; it was not a large one, but he knew at once that it was a slave ship, and so he went and told the captain. Now the captain was very glad; he did not say that because it was only a small ship it was not worth while to try and take it. No, he knew better; perhaps he thought how unhappy he should feel if he were a slave; perhaps he fancied he could see the miserable faces of the poor creatures on board, and hear their groans; anyhow he said directly that he would turn round and try and overtake the African ship, and set the poor prisoners free.

So they turned round; and when the captain of the slave ship saw that they were coming after him, he was very much afraid, for he knew that it was no use trying to get away, the other ship was so much larger, and could sail so much faster than his; and he knew, too, that it would be impossible for him with so few men to fight with the English sailors; and so what do you think he did? Why he and his men got out their boat, and they all made haste into it, and rowed away as fast as they could towards the shore.

The captain was very pleased to see them do this, for he did not want *them* at all; it was the slaves that were down in the bottom of the ship that he wanted; and they were all safe there still. So after a little while the beautiful English man-of-war, as the great ship was called, came close up to the slave ship; and then the captain sent a very kind officer and some sailors to go and take possession of it, and to take the chains off the slaves and make them as happy as they could.

But what do you think the good officer saw when he climbed up the side of the ship, and stood upon the deck? Not a great many black men and black women chained together; no, there was not one man or woman on board; but wherever he turned the officer saw little black children, some almost under his feet, some peeping out from behind heaps of sails and ropes, some on the cabin stairs, and some in the cabin itself. Wherever he looked he saw a little black face, grinning with delight that the cruel men had gone, and that the white men whom they saw looked so very kind, and so very different altogether. And very kind they were as you may be sure, and the little children had great reason to be happy; but they did not know then what they afterwards learnt, that it was the great God who took pity on them, and who sent the English captain to save them from their cruel masters.

ANON   *True Stories for Little People*, 1865

Fishing Boats—near Hastings.

The Slave's Appeal

Happy littel English childer!
Driber's whip you nebber felt!
You in homes so gay and gladsome,
For poor slaves your heart should melt;
Oh, send message to our mas'rs,
Right across de salt sea wave;
Pray dem for the lub of Jesus,
Break de chains from off de slave.

'J.E.S.'   *The Children's Friend*, January 1865

Chinese Tracts in the West Indies

Many of the Chinese labourers have emigrated to the West Indies, hoping to better their circumstances, the population of their own country being so great, that they found it difficult to obtain the necessaries of life.

They are remarkable for their industry and patient endurance of suffering.

They are usually bound to eight years' service, at four dollars a month, and are highly prized by the cultivators of the sugar plantations.

We hope that our juvenile friends will feel an interest, not only in sending Bibles and tracts, in the Chinese language, for distribution amongst these labourers, but also in helping to send Missionaries to preach to them the glorious Gospel of Christ. As we understand that the Chinese are very fond of pictures, we intend sending a parcel of the *Children's Friend* for distribution amongst the children of these emigrants from China.

ANON   *The Children's Friend*, July 1865

'The Negroes have black skins' (See page 257)

LIST OF ILLUSTRATIONS

Illustrators (*del*) and engravers (*sc*) are named when known and the original medium is stated, unless it is wood engraving printed in black and white. The size of originals is stated in millimetres, height first. Measurements refer to the pictorial surface reproduced, or outer border of the illustration, if one is included.

COLOUR

BLACK AND WHITE

LIST OF ILLUSTRATIONS

HEARTH AND HOME

POVERTY AND RICHES

LIST OF ILLUSTRATIONS

LIST OF ILLUSTRATIONS

This is in two parts: first, anonymous works; second, the works
of authors or editors whose names appear in the books listed.
All the books quoted are illustrated editions.
Books are published in London unless otherwise stated.
Undated works are identified by the abbreviation n.d.: RTS—
Religious Tract Society: SPCK—Society for the Promotion of
Christian Knowledge.

ANON. [MARTIN, WILLIAM?] *A Birthday Gift for Boys and Girls*.
Darton & Co. 1861.

ANON. *The Boy's Own Book: a complete encyclopedia of all the
diversions, athletic, scientific and recreative, of boyhood and youth*.
D. Bogue. 1855.

ANON. *The Boy's Own Book: a complete encyclopaedia of sports
and pastimes; athletic, scientific, and recreative*. Crosby Lockwood
& Co. 1878. New Edition revised and enlarged.

ANON. CHARLES, UNCLE [Pseud.] *The Boy's Book of Sports and
Games, containing rules and directions for the practice of the
principal recreative amusements of youth*. T. Allman & Son. n.d.
[inscr. 1861.] Illustrated by Henry Sears.

ANON. *The Boy's Own Treasury . . . forming a complete repertory
of home amusements and healthful recreations*. Ward & Lock.
1860.

ANON. *Charlie's Discoveries: or, a good use for eyes and ears*.
Harvey and Darton. n.d. New Edition. Illustrated by Joseph
Pitman. Engraved by Thomas Williams.

ANON. PARLEY, PETER [Pseud.] *Cheerful Cherry; or, make the
best of it. With other tales*. Darton & Co. 1863.

ANON. *The Children's Friend*. Seeley & Co. Also S. W. Partridge.
May 1865. [New series.] Volume V.

ANON. *The Children's Friend*. Seeley, Jackson & Halliday. Also
S. W. Partridge. April 1868. [New series.] Volume VIII.

ANON. *The Children's Pleasure Book: containing original tales,
biographies, and Sunday readings*. Virtue, Spalding & Daldy.
1874.

ANON. *The Children's Sunday Album*. Cassell, Petter & Galpin.
London, Paris and New York. n.d. By the author of *A Trap to
Catch a Sunbeam*.

ANON. *The Child's Companion and Juvenile Instructor*. RTS.
1860 and 1861. New series.

ANON. *Choice Poetry for Little Children*. RTS. n.d. [1871?]

ANON. *The Christmas Tree: a book of instruction and amusement
for all young people*. James Blackwood. 1857.

ANON. *The Church Missionary Juvenile Instructor*. Seeley,
Jackson and Halliday. Also Hatchard & Co. Also J. Nisbet &
Co. 1865. Volume I. New series.

ANON. *Cottage at the Firs*. RTS. London, Manchester, Brighton. n.d

ANON. *Faithful Words for Old and Young.* Alfred Holness. n.d.
[1880–81.]
ANON. *Flowers and their Teachings.* RTS. n.d. By the author of
Sunshine and Shadows in Kattern's Life.
ANON. *Footprints of Popery; or, places where martyrs have
suffered.* RTS. n.d. [Inscr. 1868.]
ANON. *Green's Nursery Annual.* Darton & Co. 1848. [Second
year.]
ANON. *Happy Children's Pets.* Darton & Co. n.d. [Inscr. 1863.]
ANON. [VALENTINE, LAURA (Jewry)]. *Home for the Holidays.*
Aunt Louisa's London toy books, No. 35. Frederick Warne &
Co. n.d. [c. 1870.] Illustrated by W. H. Petherick.
ANON. *Hungering and Thirsting.* RTS. n.d. By the author of
Willie and Lucie at the Seaside and *Charity's Birthday Text.*
ANON. JOSEPHINE [Pseud.] *Jottings for Juveniles. In simple
verse. Affectionately inscribed to the children of England.*
Houlston & Wright. 1862.
ANON. [WALTON, Mrs. O. F.] *Little Dot and her Friends and other
stories.* RTS. n.d. [Inscr. 1882.] Contains *Little Dot's daisies;
The story of Jack and Nell; The story of Little Pippin;* and *The
little lamb.*
ANON. [NEWCOMBE, SAMUEL.] *Little Henry's Holiday at the
Great Exhibition.* Houlston & Stoneman. n.d. [1851.] By the
editor of *Pleasant Pages.*
ANON. *The Little Learner's Toy Book.* RTS. n.d. [Inscr. 1878.]
ANON. N., A.R. *Little Seymour Street; or, Elsie Feltham.* SPCK.
n.d. By the author of *Woodberry Farm* and *Margaret Vere,* etc.
ANON. [PRENTISS, ELIZABETH (PAYSON).] *Little Susy's Six
Teachers.* Nelson, London, Edinburgh, New York. 1879.
[American authoress 1818–1878.] Authoress of *Stepping
Heavenward; Flowers of the Family,* etc.
ANON. *Morals from the Churchyard; in a series of cheerful fables.*
Chapman & Hall. 1838. Illustrated by H. K. Browne.
ANON. *A Mother's Lessons on Kindness to Animals.* S. W.
Partridge. n.d. New edition. [Inscr. 1865.]
ANON. *The National Nursery Book.* London. Frederick Warne &
Co. New York, Scribner, Welford & Armstrong. n.d. [c. 1872.]
ANON. *Nellie Grey; or, the ups and downs of every-day life.*
Frederick Warne & Co. n.d. New edition.
ANON. *The Nursery Times; or, stories about little ones, by an old
nurse.* Griffith & Farran. n.d. Illustrated by J. Lawson.
ANON. *Nuts and Crackers for Christmas.* London: Sunday School
Union. New York: Thomas Nelson. n.d.
ANON. [TAYLOR, JANE and GILBERT, ANN (TAYLOR).]
Original Poems. George Routledge & Sons. London and New
York. 1868. [Original edition 1804–1805.]

BIBLIOGRAPHY

ANON. *The Parent's Cabinet of Amusement and Instruction.*
Smith, Elder & Co. 1859. New edition; and 1868, New edition.
ANON. *Parlour Magic.* Tilt and Bogue. n.d. [Inscr. 1847.] To the
lovers of home this little manual of amusing phenomena for
family recreation is respectfully dedicated.
ANON. [MORTIMER, FAVELL LEE.] *The Peep of Day; or, a series
of the earliest religious instruction the infant mind is capable of
receiving.* Hatchard & Co. 1860. Revised.
ANON. *Peter Parley's Annual, a Christmas or New Year's Present
for Young People.* Simpkin, Marshall & Co. 1842.
ANON. *Peter Parley's Magazine. A Christmas and New Year
Present for Young People.* Darton & Clark. 1845.
ANON. *Peter Parley's Annual.* Darton & Co. 1852, 1854, 1856,
1857, 1868.
ANON. *Peter Parley's Familiar Tales: in illustration of natural
philosophy.* William Tegg. 1864. (4th edition).
ANON. *The Picture Scrap Book.* RTS. n.d. [Inscr. 1863.] New
series.
ANON. *Pictures for Our Pets. Home and country scenes, etc.* RTS.
n.d.
ANON. *Pictures from the Street.* [DALZIEL?] n.d. Illustrated by
W. McConnell. Engraved by Dalziel.
ANON. *Pleasant Tales for Little People.* Thomas Dean. n.d.
Contains *Anne and Jane, Sunshine and twilight, The trial of
charity, Squire Grey's fruit feast,* and *Things in their right places.*
ANON. *The Poll Parrot Picture Book.* London and New York.
George Routledge & Sons. n.d. Contains *Titmus and Fido, Ann
and her mamma, Reynard the fox, The cats' tea party.*
ANON. *The Proverbs of Solomon.* Aunt Louisa's Sunday picture
books, No. 2. Frederick Warne & Co. n.d.
ANON. PRIMOGENITA [Pseud.] *Recollections of Childhood; or,
Sally, the faithful nurse.* London: Hatchard & Sons, Seeley,
Rivingtons. Canterbury: Ward. Bristol: Light and Riddler and
Chilcott. 1840. Author a contributor to the *Penny Sunday
reader.*
ANON. *Spring Flowers and Summer Blossoms for the Young and
Good.* Thomas Dean & Son. n.d. [Inscr. 1850.] Contains: *The
snow-drop, May flowers, The wall flower, cowslips and primroses,
The hare-bells, The bee-orchis, The hyacinth, The white violets.*
ANON. *Steenie Alloway's Adventures.* RTS. n.d. [Inscr. 1882.]
ANON. *Sunday Afternoons with Mamma. A book for very little
children.* RTS. n.d. [1866.] By the author of *A visit to aunt
Agnes* [1864.]
ANON. *Tales and Stories selected from the supplemental catalogue
of the SPCK.* Parts I and II in one volume. SPCK. 1847.
ANON. *The Town and Country Toy Book.* RTS. n.d.

BIBLIOGRAPHY

ANON. *True Stories for Little People, Grave and Gay*. Seeley, Jackson and Halliday. 1865. By the author of *Little Animals*.

ABBOTT, JACOB. *Religion and Happiness: or, fire-side piety, and the duties and enjoyments of domestic devotion*. Edward Lacey. n.d. [American author 1803–79.]
ARTHUR, T. S. *Home Scenes and Home Influences. A series of tales and sketches*. Edinburgh and New York. Nelson. 1866. With illustrations by W. Small, engraved by Williamson.
ARTHUR, T. S. *Our Little Harry, and other poems and stories*. Halifax Milner & Sowerby. 1855. Illustrated by Croome.

BARBAULD, Mrs. *Hymns in Prose for Children*. John Murray. 1880. [First published in 1781.]
BISHOP, JAMES. *A Visit to the Zoological Gardens*. Dean. n.d. 6th edition. [First published by Dean and Munday. c. 1830.]
BLAIR, REV. DAVID [PHILLIPS, SIR RICHARD.] *The Mother's Question Book, containing things necessary to be known at an early age*. Darton & Co. n.d. Second series.
BRUCE, CARLTON. *The Boy's Friend; or, the maxims of a cheerful old man*. Grant & Griffith. n.d. [Inscr. 1844.] Second edition.
BUCK, RUTH. *Midsummer Holiday*. London and Edinburgh. W. & R. Chambers. n.d.
BUTLER, Mrs. C. (Ed.). *The Pleasant Verse and Prose Coloured Picture Story Book*. Thomas Dean & Son. n.d. Contains 3 vols. *The public buildings of London; Tales of the months and seasons; Trees, fruits and flowers*.
BYRNE, JANET. *Picture Teaching for Young and Old*. Cassell, Petter and Galpin. n.d. [Inscr. 1881.]

CHILD, Mrs. *The Girl's Own Book*. William Tegg. 1848. (14th edition).
CLARKE, J. ERSKINE (Ed.). *The Children's Prize*. W. W. Gardner. June 1873.

EDGEWORTH, MARIA. *The Bracelets* and *The Good French Governess*. Houlston & Wright. 1868. New edition. *The Good French Governess* first appeared in *Moral Tales for Young People*. 1801.

GELDART, Mrs. THOMAS. *The Nursery Guide, and Infant's First Hymn Book. An original work for children from three to six years of age*. London: R. Yorke Clarke (successors to Harvey & Darton). Also, Norwich: J. Fletcher, and Jarrold & Sons. 1850. (Third edition, re-issue.)
GOODRICH, S. G. *Juvenile Forget-me-not* or *Parley's forget-me-not for the young*. Darton & Co. 1858.

HACK, MARIA. *Harry Beaufoy; or, a pupil of nature*. Darton &
Harvey. 1845. (Fifth edition.) With illustrations by T. Landseer.
[First published in 1821.]

HALL, Mrs. S. C. *The Juvenile Budget, or stories for little readers*.
Chapman & Hall. Also A. K. Newman & Co. 1840. Illustrated by
H. K. Browne.

HALL, Mrs. S. C.; TAYLOR, EMILY; CORNER, JULIA, and other
authors. *The Story Garden*. Groombridge & Sons. 1876.

HOWITT, MARY. *Tales in Prose*. Darton & Co. n.d. (Second
series.)

JERRAM, Mrs. [JANE ELIZABETH (HOLMES)]. *The Child's Own
Story Book, or tales and dialogues for the nursery*. Darton &
Clark. 1840. (Second edition.)

JOSEPHINE [Pseud.] *See* Anonymous. *Jottings for Juveniles*.

KENNEDY, GRACE. *Anna Ross: a story for children*. Edinburgh:
William Oliphant & Sons. Glasgow: W. Collins. Dublin: William
Curry. London: Hamilton, Adams & Co. 1848, Ninth edition.
[First published in 1823.]

KINGSON, AL. *The Pictorial Word Book in English and French*.
J. H. Truchy, Paris. n.d.

MARTIN, WILLIAM. *The Book of Sports; containing indoor sports,
short games, recreations, conundrums, charades, etc., for boys and
girls*. Darton & Co. 1858.

MARTIN, WILLIAM (Ed.). *The Hatchups of Me and My Schoolfellows, by Peter Parley*. Darton & Co. 1858.

MARTIN, WILLIAM (Ed.). *Peter Parley's Annual*. Darton & Co.
1858, 1867.

MARTIN, WILLIAM (Ed.). *Peter Parley's Annual*. William Kent.
1866.

MARTIN, WILLIAM (Ed.). *Peter Parley's Own Favourite Story
Book for Young People*. Charles Griffin & Co. n.d.

MAYHEW, THE BROTHERS. *Acting Charades, or deeds not words.
A Christmas game to make a long evening short*. D. Bogue. n.d.
Illustrated by H. G. Hine.

MILLER, THOMAS. *The Boy's Own Country Book, descriptive of the
seasons and rural amusements*. London and New York, George
Routledge & Sons. n.d.

MILLER, THOMAS. *The Boy's Spring Book, descriptive of the season,
scenery, rural life, and country amusements*. Chapman & Hall.
1847. With coloured illustrations by Birket Foster, engraved by
Vizetelly & Co.

MITFORD, MARY RUSSELL. *Children of the Village*. London and
New York, George Routledge & Sons. n.d.

MORTIMER, FAVELL. *See* Anonymous. *The Peep of Day*.

NEWCOMBE, SAMUEL. *See* Anonymous. *Little Henry's Holiday at the Great Exhibition.*

NEWTON, Rev. RICHARD. *The Giants, and How to Fight Them.* London, Edinburgh and New York: T. Nelson & Sons. 1875. [First published in 1863.]

PARLEY, PETER, *See* Martin, William and Anonymous works.

PATCH, OLIVE. *Familiar Friends.* Cassell, Petter and Galpin. n.d. [Inscr. 1880.]

PHILLIPS, RICHARD. *See* Blair, David.

POTTER, F. SCARLETT. *The Sexton's Grandsons.* London: SPCK. New York: Pott, Young & Co. n.d.

PRENTISS, ELIZABETH. *See* Anonymous. *Little Suzy's Six Teachers.*

PRIMOGENITA [Pseud.]. *See* Anonymous. *Recollections of Childhood.*

ROUTLEDGE, EDMUND (Ed.). *Routledge's Every Boy's Annual. An entertaining miscellany of original literature.* London and New York: Routledge, Warne & Routledge. 1863. Frontispiece and title page illuminated by Samuel Stanesby.

ROUTLEDGE, EDMUND (Ed.). *Routledge's Every Boy's Annual. An entertaining miscellany of original literature.* London and New York: George Routledge & Sons. 1871.

ROUTLEDGE, EDMUND (Ed.). *Every Boy's Book. A complete encyclopaedia of sports and amusements.* London and New York: George Routledge & Sons. 1876.

SEWELL, Mrs. *Mother's Last Words.* Jarrold & Sons. n.d.

SHERWOOD, Mrs. *The History of the Fairchild Family.* Hatchards. 1869. [First published between 1818 and 1847, in three parts.]

SHERWOOD, Mrs. *The History of the Fairchild Family, or the child's manual. Being a collection of stories calculated to show the importance and effects of a religious education.* Hatchard and G. Routledge & Sons. 1880.

SHERWOOD, Mrs. [and KELLY, SOPHIA]. *The Little Lady, and Other Stories.* Milner & Co. n.d. [Inscr. 1876.] Contains fourteen stories, six of which, including *Anno mundi*, are by SOPHIA KELLY.

SHUTTLEWORTH, Rev. H. C. (Ed.). *My Sunday Friend. An illustrated volume for children.* Oxford and London: A. R. Mowbray. 1878.

STRICKLAND, AGNES, and BARTON, BERNARD. *Fisher's Juvenile Scrap Book.* London, Paris and America: Fisher, Son & Co. 1837. Velvet binding.

STRICKLAND, AGNES. *Floral Sketches, Fables and Other Poems.* Hamilton, Adams & Co. Also Webb, Millington & Co. n.d. (New edition.)

TAYLOR, ANN and JANE. *See* Anonymous. *Original Poems.*
TEGG, THOMAS. *A Present for an Apprentice, to which is added Franklin's way of wealth.* William Tegg & Co. 1848. Second edition. With frontispiece by G. Cruickshank, engraved on steel by S. Davenport.
THORP, ANN. *Aunt Kate's Story, about the vicar and his family.* Bristol. 1845. Illustrated by R. Pocock. A. Pocock, lithographer.

VALENTINE, LAURA. *See* Anonymous. *Home for the Holidays.*

WALTON, Mrs. O. F. *See* Anonymous. *Little Dot and Her Friends.*
WATTS, ISAAC. *Divine and Moral Songs for Children.* RTS. n.d. [First published 1715.]
WATTS, JOHN G. (Selector). *Little Lays for Little Folk.* George Routledge & Sons. 1867.
WINNARD, Miss. *Fanny and Arthur: or, persevere and prosper. A tale of interest.* Dean & Son. n.d. Including hand coloured illustrations by J. V. Barnet, engraved by Harrison.
WORDSWORTH, WILLIAM. *Wordsworth's Poems for the Young.* Alexander Strahan. 1866.